growing more beautiful

growing more beautiful

AN ARTFUL APPROACH TO PERSONAL STYLE

BY JENNIFER ROBIN

ARTEFUL
PRESS

Published in the United States by Arteful Press, an imprint of Petaluma Publishing Company, Petaluma, California, 94952, growingmorebeautiful.com, artefulpress.com

ISBN 978-0-9817322-0-6

Printed in China through Global Interprint

Book design: Campana Design

contents

blossoming

When the first blossoming trees herald the arrival of spring, do more than just admire them as you drive past. Find a blooming tree and spend a few moments standing beneath it. Better yet, bring your paints or borrow your child's crayons and experiment with capturing the pinkness of the blossoms. Look up at the color of the afternoon sky. Is it dark and leaden, or are the blooms silhouetted against crisp, pure blueness? Is a breeze blowing, sending drifts of delicate petals to the ground?

Breathe in this moment of pure experience and let it soak in. The color and beauty will seep into your skin, and you will experience the same benefits as a luxurious spa treatment. Check out your face immediately afterwards. With any luck, you will have a paint smudge on your cheek. As you look in the mirror, tell me, do you see the glow?

about this book

This book is my way of sharing with you the satisfaction that is possible when you take an artful approach to personal style. This isn't a collection of platitudes about inner beauty and nature's miracles, because I know you are looking for practical, outward results, and are willing to work for them. *Growing More Beautiful: An Artful Approach to Personal Style* is a guide to savoring the pleasure of caring for your appearance, combined with an approach to overcoming the obstacles in your path. We all long to look great, but the process of getting there also needs to be a rich and rewarding experience. My goal is to show you how to care for both your inner life and your outward appearance in a way that creates that unmistakable glow we all long for.

When a makeover show claims the answer to all your style problems lies in finding the perfect pair of $300 jeans and wearing them with high heels, you know you need more and better options. Makeover shows are fun to watch, but there is no more nourishment available from them than what you get from a fat-free cookie. The sugar buzz is there, but nothing is offered to sustain you. Women are endlessly creative, both at home and in the workplace. The approach outlined in this book will help you solve problems and create beauty by calling on that part of yourself.

There have been many excellent books written about fashion and personal style, but *Growing More Beautiful* takes a new approach by seeing the process through the eyes of an artist and painter. The elements of making art, including many of the principles of design, help with any creative endeavor whether it is painting or creating an outfit.

There are no before-and-after examples in this book, no dramatically engineered makeovers to dazzle you. We have been conditioned to watch others for examples of how to look, and to endlessly compare ourselves in a way that makes us feel we are lacking. This is why I am including other artful images of paintings and photographs for your spirit to connect to. I hope some will touch you, and that you will look around for other sources of inspiration to help you develop your sense of self. The image you carry of yourself comes from within, and is generated by how you feel and think. Only you know when the image in the mirror is reflecting back to you in a satisfying way.

The vignettes about painting that begin each chapter are my way of giving you the same pause to refresh yourself that painting gives me. Encourage your own inner artist to help guide and inspire you to discover a new way of seeing, feeling and being.

In the chapters ahead you can look forward to solid information that will enhance the way you care for your appearance. Before we dive into the specifics, I want to set the stage for what lies ahead. I do this in the special section called **THE BIG IDEAS,** which contains the philosophical principles of *Growing More Beautiful*. I hope you will return to these fundamental principles if ever you feel overwhelmed or discouraged.

Other Parts of *Growing More Beautiful* focus on taking action, whether it be changing your self-talk or choosing a lipstick. The following chapters will provide a road map and the beacon of beauty to light your way.

ILLUMINATE how you look at your body and the fears and frustrations of growing older.

EXPLORE the paths to discovering your individuality. Expanding your awareness of *Color* will transform the way you look and feel. Next we move to the *Language of Personal Style*. The growing awareness you are developing about the uniqueness of your body will be further explained in the following chapter on how to determine *Style and Fit.*

PREPARE to focus on what you need from your clothes by looking at your *Lifestyle* and delving into your *Closet*. This section concludes by helping you A*fford* what you love by encouraging you to look at your financial style.

ENVISION how you want to look before you even step into the stores by creating a *Collage* or folio of images.

At last, time to **ACT**. Let's go *Shopping!*

PERSONALIZE your new clothes with *Jewelry and Accessories*.

POLISH your look with tips on *Make-up and Hair*.

GLOW as you create a more *Artful Life.* I suspect you are hungry for both inspiration and solid information. Real nourishment comes from engaging your entire self as you move forward. The upcoming chapters will lead you step-by-step through the process I've developed working with hundreds of men and women over the last twenty years and continue to use with my image consulting clients. I look forward to sharing my favorite tools and techniques with you.

Throughout the book I offer suggestions, exercises and activities to help you learn how to express your personal style. A journal with pages heavy enough for using markers or gluing items cut from magazines will come in handy for recording your insights.

growing into an artist

I'd like to share some background about how *Growing More Beautiful* came to be. In 1987, I authored the popular book, *Clothe Your Spirit: Dressing For Self-Expression* (Spirit Press). At the time, the most influential book on clothing for the professional woman was *Dress For Success* (Warner Books) by John Molloy, first published in 1976. We've come a long way since women were advised to emulate men by dressing in matched business suits complete with little bow ties.

At the beginning of the 1990s, I was busy with seminars and clients. Then illness pushed me rudely off the fashion fast track. Suddenly sidelined, I turned my attention to healing. The color palettes I created for my clients to use in building their wardrobes had always brought me joy, but I longed to burst out of the confines of color as it related to clothing choices. I dreamed of mixing orange with magenta, blue-gray with ochre, making "mud" by mixing complimentary colors to create muddy gray or brown. I wanted more from color and I craved being able to express myself more freely. I took my first tentative steps toward painting.

Slowly, like the kindergartener I was when I'd abandoned playing with brushes and paper, I began to make marks on paper. As I recovered my health, my interest in painting grew alongside my continuing work in the image field. My journey toward *Growing More Beautiful* had begun. Fifteen frustrating, challenging, engaging years later, I have only just started to venture down the path toward *learning to see*, an odyssey that will last my lifetime.

Painting has taught me lessons in process, patience, love and commitment that I can apply to all aspects of my life. While studying the human form during my weekly drawing class, I've learned how all parts relate to the whole. Discovering how the artist's eye travels the length of the body has enhanced my ability to choose flattering clothing for myself and for my clients. Painting outdoors, I've learned that true beauty comes from loving something greater than your own reflection. The experts tell me I haven't done my skin any good; I've let the hot sun burn my neck more times than I can count. But still, my reflected face is radiant, lit up by the joy that creating art brings into my life.

The day following a painting session will often find me helping a client shop for new clothes. After those hours of visual stimulation, the colors and textures in the fitting room dazzle my senses. I love my work with fashion for the way it allows artistic principles to come to life in three dimensions. If I am working on a fall wardrobe, I might use the same rich hues of eggplant and persimmon I had put into a painting the day before. Learning to see well enough to capture the breadth of a landscape has refined my eye as well as opened my consciousness.

In the years since I have regained my health, I have continued to be mindful of my need to create balance in order to stay healthy. I've found that making art helps offset the superficial nature of the fashion world. Painting and writing allow me the solitude I need for reflection so I can jump back into the dynamic fashion arena with a fresh perspective. A broader viewpoint also does wonders for distracting the inner critic. Like an endless waterfall, my connection to the creative process renews my energy and makes all aspects of life flow more easily.

I continue to strengthen the most important attribute of all, my intuition. During the time I was recovering from being ill, I relearned the "magic words." Not "please" and "thank you," but the physical experience of "Yes!" and "No!" "No," my body says, "Stop! I don't want to go there," or "Yes, let's move forward, I'm excited." Learning to listen to the fundamental language of the inner voice is the key to strengthening your intuition. A connection to your intuitive voice is crucial in defining for yourself what you consider truly beautiful.

the big picture

After several hectic days of shopping, searching for accessories and assembling outfits, my client Barbara posed the question, "With all the difficulties in the world today, how do we reconcile so much emphasis on appearance?"

My answer is that in each of us resides a deep desire to be seen. We long for our beauty to be expressed in such a way that others will glimpse our essence. It is as natural as breathing to want to see the beauty of all you are reflected back at you. The longing we feel to be beautiful is as inherent as our desire for any of our other unique qualities to be seen and appreciated.

Don't shy away from being all that you are. Assert your right to be unique, to have your own style. The choices you make shape the world your daughters and sons will grow up in. Who you are matters to your neighbors, the community and the world.

Finding the best way to express yourself through your appearance is a journey worth taking. This book is dedicated to helping you find the road that will lead you to taking pleasure in your own reflection.

"Somehow nice clothing is an optimistic anchor to the beauty of this life." SANDRA

THE ART OF PERSONAL STYLE

Learning to see and understand your essence is a lifelong process.

Learning to express your essence with clothing is a daily act of creation.

getting the glow

We all notice a woman who has a visible passion for life. The beauty and confidence she radiates is unmistakable. Her clear skin, shiny hair, radiant smile, elegant posture and springy step are all part of her glow. We all know how important it is to maintain our health and well-being, to rest, eat right and use great skincare. Certainly good concealer and lipstick help, but your glow comes from your aliveness, from giving yourself permission to do things your own way.

The good news is, your spirit is unquestionably beautiful! The most important criteria of being a beautiful person is caring deeply about others. I hope you feel a passion for life, and that you greet your days with vitality and excitement. Whom you love, what you feel connected to, and your attitude about yourself are the essential foundation of your beauty.

One of the catchy titles suggested for this book was Getting the Glow, but "the glow" isn't something you "get." It is something that returns to you, like a promise, or an affirmation that you are living in a way that supports your true essence.

I know from personal experience that "the glow" is not something I can take for granted. When I am off track, pushing too hard, doubting myself, not putting my well-being first, my glow vanishes. When I spend more time caught in the whirl of shopping than I do painting or in nature, my outfit might look nice, but my glow is in serious jeopardy.

The glow takes maintenance and, in this case, it is the maintenance of your spirit. You have to chart your own course and make your own rules because there are no absolute beauty guidelines to follow. Everything I write about in this book helps to make the glow happen, but is not a formula. It only works if you do it with your own flair.

The feeling of being beautiful arises when you feel a connection to all those around you and to the whole of life itself. As you move through life, it is not only possible, but natural, to grow more beautiful.

learning to see

Becoming an artist is a process of *learning to see*. As a painter struggles to represent an image, she must remind herself over and over that this painting is but a moment in a lifelong journey of learning to see. Therefore, if you are the work of art, the canvas to embellish, that expression begins with learning to see yourself clearly.

Learning to see yourself clearly is as elusive as looking into a pond's reflection on a breezy day. As we learn to look without judgment, and be present for what is before us, the wind drops and the image becomes clearer and more focused.

Who is the shimmering reflection that you see in the surface of a pool? The image wavers and blurs as wind fans ripple across the water. Then in a moment of stillness and calm, there you are, clearer and more visible, seeing this version of yourself as if for the first time.

Who is this person I am growing more and more intimate with?

If beauty is in the eye of the beholder, then behold yourself.

the critical voice

What clouds our vision? For some artists, the critical inner voice can be so potent that they give up making art forever. In our culture, feeling critical of our looks is what we wake up to each morning for breakfast.

Is it any surprise we can't see ourselves clearly? A single beauty standard is pervasive and accepted without question. We are expected to be on an endless quest for perfection in the form of slim, taut bodies; sculptured, dewy, unlined faces; thick, shiny hair; and eternal youthfulness. Everywhere we turn, we are promised secrets to attaining this level of perfection. In our hearts we know that beauty doesn't exist on the pages of glossy magazines, but we read them anyway, not necessarily seeking beauty tips, but looking for something we can relate to. Going beyond beauty advice, you can strengthen your inner life, fill it with a creative fire that incinerates the critic and allows you to move beyond belittling yourself and judging others.

When you remove the invasive weeds of self-doubt and shame that are choking your true essence, you will blossom like a tree that is being nurtured and cared for, Growing More Beautiful with each passing season.

choices

Gray hair started showing up in my dark locks in my twenties, and now that I am fifty, I am mostly silver. An afternoon and a bottle of dark hair dye could change that. For a variety of reasons, I've *chosen* to have my hair stay its natural color. For me, gray hair is an issue of choice rather than aging.

There are so many different ways to care for your appearance. To color or not color your hair is one of many options you get to consider as you choose to care for your appearance in the way that is right for you. The challenge is to find the combination that suits you. How you see yourself will be transformed when you approach looking your best in a way that reflects your personal values. Deciding what matters to you and what you believe in, and standing behind it, is what makes the choices authentically yours.

If you hate the gym, find some form of exercise that will lift your spirits. If you are sick of coloring your hair, stop. If wearing high heeled shoes is painful torture, then throw them away. Don't do the things you dislike.

Once you stop doing what you loathe (all the beauty "shoulds"), ask yourself what you enjoy. I, for one, love new clothes, make-up, haircuts, brilliantly painted toenails, walking and dancing. I have clients who love the gym, yoga and getting their hair highlighted. Some even swear by botox injections, waxing appointments or silent meditation retreats. We're all different.

Here's the bottom line: Doing something that you do not enjoy does not make you more beautiful. Choosing what makes you happy creates a sense of wholeness and confidence that is unmistakable.

like attracts like

The big leap is having faith in your choices. When you make choices that are true to who you are, there is the fear that being you will not be enough. If you put your true self out into the world, there is always the possibility there will be no takers.

In fact, the opposite is true. The next time you are in a gathering of people, turn off your comparison radar in favor of open-minded curiosity. We're trained to be competitive, but making judgments pulls you away from others instead of allowing your true self to come forward. Look for that mutual spark of commonality as a way to make a connection.

When you are authentically yourself, like-minded people will find you and be attracted to you. Once you understand this, there is tremendous relief in knowing you can't appear attractive to everyone, or even be seen by everyone.

beautiful and sexy

When you express your essence, others *see* you. Great-fitting clothes in gorgeous colors, worn with pride and self-confidence, will make heads turn. Be aware of how you move in your clothes and how your clothes move with you. Learn what is unique about you, and then highlight it.

Looking sexy is not about wearing revealing clothes. Sexiness is being conscious of what you find beautiful about your face and figure, and then showing that to the world. If you focus on camouflaging every ripple of flesh and scrap of fat, what others will see is self-consciousness, not sexiness.

You can't reach your full sexiness potential if you are worried about what others will think of you. Being beautiful (and sexy) is about showing up in all your glory.

love of learning

My first painting instructor taught me to value myself as a painter, to appreciate my original way of applying paint and my unique vision. Without her encouragement, I never would have been able to persevere through the awkward moments of being a beginner.

As time went on, being "expressive" wasn't enough. I craved more information. When I started painting with my current instructor, I didn't understand her teaching style. Why was she picking such boring locations? Why only rolling hills and cow pastures populated by the occasional oak or eucalyptus? It turned out that understanding the structure of the land itself is a foundational skill for a landscape painter. In order to communicate with paint more clearly, I needed to learn the fundamentals of shape and form. Now I've gathered some of the tools I need to move forward, and both the process and results have become more satisfying.

Knowledge doesn't stifle creativity; it enhances it. If you are drawn to something and find yourself doing it intuitively, learning about the principles behind it make the experience richer. Things make sense. Soon after you understand the theory it becomes subtext, and you can create in a more relaxed way.

In the chapters ahead, you will be reading about the artistic principles that apply both to painting and creating an outfit or wardrobe, including: *shape, texture, scale, center of interest, color, proportion, movement, unifying elements, contrast, balance and focal point.*

You can look forward to using these tools to broaden your experience and enhance your satisfaction.

Understanding the lay of the fashion and beauty landscape and learning the necessary fundamentals will help guide you toward the results you desire.

Surround yourself with beautiful fabric.

pleasure, passion and perseverance

Along your path, pleasure is the oasis where you stop and savor the experience. Since your appearance will never be a finished product, seek out and enjoy the pleasurable aspects of tending to your beauty. Surrounding yourself with beautiful fabric, experimenting with luscious lipsticks, and ridding yourself of clothing you have never enjoyed are all rewarding in the moment and prepare you for future delights.

There are times where the shopping trip is hellish, nothing fits, and you haven't been able to find anything you like after hours of searching. I've had many similar moments both as a consultant and an artist. I still wince hearing stories of my client's disappointments, or remembering my own frustration the afternoon I tried to capture a late harvest pumpkin patch in a painting, only to be told the results looked like oranges or, worse yet, basketballs.

The negative experiences make you wonder why you bother but if you are passionate about something, you stick with it. The reason you continue lies in your commitment to doing something that matters to you.

Discover the many pleasurable aspects of caring for your appearance and your spirit.
Learn what is holding you back so you can continue to move forward.
Use your passion to overcome obstacles. Persevere.

Part One ILLUMINATE

perfect in its wholeness

〜〜〜〜〜〜〜〜〜〜〜〜〜〜〜〜〜〜〜〜〜〜〜〜〜〜〜〜〜〜〜〜〜

Rain pelts the tin roof of our drawing studio. Our class has arranged our easels to form a circle around a voluptuous nude model posing on a raised platform.

We start with quick poses, charcoal sketches on newsprint, big bold gestures to awaken our eyes and hands.

We move on to the long poses, dipping our brushes into wet, juicy paint, attempting to capture skin tones, patterns of light and dark that slowly reveal themselves as shape and form. My hand and eyes merge into one, as do the curves of the model, each one flowing into the next, an organization of shapes perfect in its wholeness.

I've noticed that when we have a fuller female model everyone breathes easier, because for those few hours we are all allowed to enjoy the pleasure of looking at sensuous fleshy curves. As we take in the lushness, we are healing our own inner critics, awakening to the experience that all forms in nature are beautiful.

body image

⤬⤬⤬⤬⤬⤬⤬⤬⤬⤬⤬⤬⤬⤬⤬⤬⤬⤬⤬⤬⤬⤬⤬⤬⤬⤬⤬⤬⤬⤬⤬⤬⤬⤬⤬⤬⤬

SEE YOURSELF IN A NEW LIGHT

Here's my guess: you have your image of the perfect woman. If you've ever seen a line drawing of a steer with dotted marks outlining the different cuts of meat, imagine a similar rendering of your ideal woman. Her arms, shoulders, breasts, belly, hips, thighs, calves, hands and feet are the gold standard you measure yourself against. You rate your own body to see how close it comes to this perceived ideal. Your stomach may pass muster, but your arms and buttocks are too full. Your legs and shoulders might be okay, but everything in between needs improvement. You are incapable of seeing your body as an integrated whole, in perfect balance and harmony with itself.

The fact that our culture has a dangerously limited idea of what constitutes physical beauty is not a revelation to most of us, yet we still struggle to accept the size and shape of our own bodies. Even if we know intellectually that the images plastered on magazine covers are unrealistic, it is still difficult not to compare them to whatever shape our bodies happen to be in now.

Improving your body image begins when you can focus on your assets instead of your perceived imperfections. Finding aspects of your body to admire and, in turn, highlighting them with clothing, is a great first step. Going one step further, you can learn to see your body in its entirety, one curve flowing into the integrated and superbly proportioned whole. *Growing More Beautiful* begins with changing your attitude to one that is healthier and more realistic, surrounding yourself with like-minded people who share your beliefs, and *learning to see yourself in a new way*.

BEAUTIFULLY IN BALANCE

The way your body is put together is lyrical, like a melody. With any piece of art, you need to be able to see the parts in relationship to the whole.

Let me tell you about some experiences that reshaped my vision. A number of years ago, I

You can learn to see your body in its entirety,
one curve flowing into the integrated whole.

I now encourage each of my clients to see how her body forms a beautifully balanced, intelligent, integrated whole.

started taking figure drawing classes. Each week we had a different live, naked model, and I was to capture its likeness on my drawing pad. At first, all I could see were parts: breasts, bellies, buttocks, nipples, strangely foreign male genitalia. Distinctive features were the only thing my untrained eye could focus on. "Proportion, proportion," my instructor Carol would say over and over. "Gage the length of the torso, notice how the pelvis sits, look how the shoulder attaches to the collarbone." I began to see how every connection mattered. My eyes needed to make hundreds of tiny measurements as I learned the landscape of each particular model's body. In those early days, my torsos were invariably too long and took up the entire page. The breasts and thighs were too prominent. "Try to learn to see inside," Carol instructed. Or she handed me a stick and a bottle of ink and said, "Stop thinking and just look. Sketch what you see."

Learning to see the whole instead of the parts seemed to be what was required. As I slowly began to learn this skill in class, I started to wonder if I could learn to see myself as I was starting to see the models. As an image consultant, I had come to see the body as a collection of assets and fit challenges, areas to emphasize and areas to downplay. *Now I was learning that the secret to understanding form was seeing all parts and proportions as a unified whole.* After class I would go home and squint at my reflection in a full-length mirror, trying to imagine my body in front of my group, viewed in its entirety instead of the limited, sidelong way I had always looked at it.

Over time I stopped seeing those models as disjointed "parts" and started seeing more unity. When you looked at my drawings you could actually recognize the model. My view of my own body began to transform as well, ever so slowly moving from acceptance to appreciation. I occasionally flip back into the old negative view, seeing my "flaws" in a disjointed, exaggerated way. But this new way of seeing has enhanced my ability to choose flattering and expressive clothing. A greater connection to my physical form allows me to connect even more fully with my essence.

I don't expect you to take up figure drawing in order to learn to see and understand the beauty of your body, but I do hope you'll dedicate yourself to the process of learning to see yourself in a more positive light. To learn to see the good, you have to be willing to look. You don't see only with your eyes, but with your mind, your heart and your life experience. Open up to the possibilities of feeling more loving and appreciative of the image you see in the mirror.

I now encourage each of my clients to see how her body forms a beautifully balanced, intelligent, integrated whole. I always tell her so, even though she rarely believes me. The harsh critic in the mirror drowns out my voice, but sometimes the door opens just a crack and a little light shines into the darkness.

PRACTICE BEING POSITIVE

Many of my clients are courageous, but none braver than Shelley. When we went shopping for a bathing suit, she completely put her trust in me. For a young, curvy size 16 with a great attitude, a boring black one-piece would not do. Shelley has generous hips and thighs and an attractive midriff, making her a perfect candidate for a two-piece swimsuit.

The winner that day was a terrific red JAG bikini that fit her perfectly. "Okay," she said hesitantly, "but I'm not sure I can wear this around my family. My mother isn't as comfortable with my weight as I am. She thinks I should be smaller."

Shelley purchased the red suit, as well as a few other great choices. Several weeks later I worried I might have pushed her too far, so I called her to check. She left me a message, and here are her exact words:

"The bathing suit has been a hit. I'm all about bikinis. I feel so much better in them; it is like the comfort and confidence I have being naked. I've always felt more comfortable without clothes than I do in a bathing suit. Now when I see a boring 'hide yourself' black one-piece I think, 'Oh, how sad, what a sad thing.' I love the red one so much that I wear it to do yard work. I feel like when I met you I was a cement block, and that you have chipped away at the concrete until my beauty was exposed."

My attitude about bathing suits: Don't apologize. Take off your clothes and put on some attitude. Don't try to hide inside a "miracle slim suit." It won't work. Forget trying to choose something that changes your shape. Don't allow yourself to be squeezed smaller — expand into your essence. In a swimsuit you are close to being naked, your body shows. You can't cover it up, so emphasize what is beautiful about it. No apologies.

You can update your attitude before you set foot into a fitting room. Shelley had done some terrific work on her self-image before she met me. She is also conscious of spending time with friends who are like-minded and dating guys who are appropriately appreciative.

When you are buying a bathing suit, remind yourself that you will not be wearing it for a layout in a fashion magazine. If I were posing for some before-and-after profile on bathing suits and middle-aged women, I'd probably wear a sleek maillot. But I'm not posing for a magazine, I'm going somewhere tropical with my husband who likes seeing what he calls, my "delicious body" exposed. If he wants to pick out a brightly colored bikini for me, I'll give him the pleasure of my wearing it. No camera is posed to take a "before" shot of me showing my-none-too-flat stomach, and no one on the beach in Tahiti is there to judge me. If you are going to a resort where you feel there will be a lot of body judging going on, then that's your call. But try asking yourself who's judging whom?

Cultivate compassion for your sisters out there. Very few of them feel all that great about exposing their tender bodies to judgmental eyes. As you send them a silent message of support, imagine you are receiving one in return. Then go and enjoy the feel of warmth and water on your skin.

Cultivate compassion for your sisters out there. Very few of them feel all that great about exposing their tender bodies to judgmental eyes. As you send them a silent message of support, imagine you are receiving one in return. Then go and enjoy the feel of warmth and water on your skin.

ENVIRONMENTAL IMPACT

The people you surround yourself with make a difference in your self-image. Obviously, you want to avoid anyone who says unkind things or is directly critical of you. Usually the slights and put downs we experience are more subtle. You can't always choose whom you come in contact with, but you can be aware of their influence.

My clients come in every conceivable shape and size, from 2P to 22W and beyond. Jill is unusual in that she has the toned, shapely physique one usually only sees in Hollywood. Jill works very hard to stay in shape, and it shows. I have many clients with lovely figures, but I've noticed that only when I've spent time with Jill do I come home feeling frumpy and lumpy.

On one of our shopping trips, we had a conversation about the trend of robust young women showing off their bellies with low pants and tight tops. I told her, "More power to them. Hopefully they will grow up to be more confident about their bodies than I am about mine."

"Well," Jill said, "I think it is disgusting! Don't they look in the mirror?" She went on to tell me about full-figured women wearing bikinis and other outbreaks of flesh she finds appalling. I cringed inwardly, hoping I wouldn't run into her in Hawaii.

The day we had this conversation, low-rise pants were just coming into fashion, and I was feeling daring enough to try a pair, the curve of my soft belly showing through my slightly sheer tucked-in top. I remember liking how I felt when I left the house in the morning, stylish and spunky. The top looked much better tucked into the top of my waistband, but after a morning with Jill I had untucked it because I felt I had something to hide.

Jill feels a lot of pressure to look a certain way and maintain her image. She is harder on herself than anyone else. It is difficult not to be impacted by that when you are around her. I know what I believe and what matters to me, but that doesn't mean I'm not susceptible to someone else's critical attitude, especially in an area where any woman feels vulnerable. Since that day, I've decided that shopping days with Jill are not the time to take fashion risks, and I make sure to wear an outfit I am especially comfortable in. After a day of shopping together I might be badgered by self-critical demons, but I know that the feeling will pass, and it soon does. I remind myself that as much as I like Jill, we have different attitudes toward our appearance.

Many of my clients are more accepting than Jill, and I learn from their example. Connie is truly comfortable with herself. A couple of months ago, she asked me to come over and help her go through her closet. Connie had gained about fifteen pounds since our last big shopping trip two years ago. We spent the afternoon moving

all the things that we still loved but were too small into another closet. She tried everything on without denigrating herself. When we were finished, we had a realistic idea of what she had and what she needed.

When we went shopping, the outfits we found were as bold and expressive as ever. "I was afraid I would have to compromise because of the extra weight," Connie said, "But I was delighted I didn't have to. Everything looked great."

"I'm well-loved," she said. "My husband and family love me just as much at this weight. I'm fortunate enough that I can afford to buy new clothes. I had a hard year, nursing my father through a long illness and grieving his death. Food was my comfort. I'm still not ready to start dieting in earnest, but I want to take care of myself. It was so frustrating staring into my closet and seeing all those clothes, not knowing what fit and what didn't. Now I feel I've moved forward."

I've heard similar post-closet cleaning sentiments before, but I noticed how her attitude made me feel more relaxed, gave me permission to be a little easier with myself. So what if my outfit wasn't perfect that day, or if my shoes or handbag weren't the latest thing? It was truly pleasant to be around her. We long for people in our life who make us feel this way, and we can begin by acting that way towards ourselves.

When we don't judge ourselves harshly, we don't judge others. When we open our hearts to others, everyone benefits. When we are kind to ourselves, everyone else feels more relaxed, breathes more easily.

I hate to end this section on a down note, but there is one more story that begs to be told. Remember Shelley in the red bikini? Shelley began feeling so good about herself that she asked if we could include her mother on one of our shopping trips. "I want to educate Mom on the process I do with you. I want her to see where I am now, how I jump up and down when I find the perfect thing. I want her to see my enthusiasm and self-confidence, to know who I am. Clothes and shopping is one of the languages women speak, and we haven't spoken it that well together."

Can you see where this is heading? I had the same sinking feeling. I agreed to make a shopping date, but warned her not to set her expectations too high. "It might not be possible for your mom to see you the way you are learning to see yourself," I said. "Her life experience has taken her to a different place."

Sure enough, the day was not a great success. Seeing bubbly, effervescent Shelley with her mother was like opening a can of soda and watching it go flat before your eyes. Everything that fit Shelley properly her mother thought was too small. Finally, I decided we had all had enough, and ended the appointment. It was a disappointing day for Shelley, but I am happy to report she was back to her spunky self in no time.

When you allow someone into the fitting room with you, choose wisely. Only supportive and helpful companions are allowed. Immediately leave a store if the sales staff makes you feel uncomfortable. I wish I could tell you to check your inner critic at the door, but that isn't always possible. If something has stirred up the little demon and it is going berserk, slam the door in its face and return to the fitting room another day. The influences that surround you will impact you, but you are still free to choose what you believe in and value.

Long term insecurity and growing confidence can exist side by side. The negative voice isn't ever really silenced. It plays in your ear as half of your mental stereo sound system. In one ear is the critic, in the other a more positive commentary, the voice of love, affirmation and pleasure. Turn up the pleasure volume and it will consistently drown out the negative voice, but be assured that the critic will continue to add its rude two cents.

Learning to see yourself in a positive way is a process. The important thing is that you are moving forward. Embrace who you are now, and all you are becoming.

MOVING TOWARD A BETTER BODY IMAGE

If you find yourself longing to look like the slender celebrity you see in a magazine, ask yourself if she is really beautiful or just familiar. Do you really think flat stomachs and muscular arms are aesthetic? We are so used to looking at clothes on rail-thin bodies that we think of it as the norm. Watching a fleshy Marilyn Monroe in *Some Like It Hot* will remind you how accustomed we have become to the bone-thinness of today's screen actresses. Do you feel your heart open when you look at images of rounder, fuller women? The lushness of women painted by Renoir, Degas, Cassatt and the other Impressionists are like poetry for the eyes.

Maybe you like the look of super-toned bodies, but ask yourself if you want to spend that much time working on yours. Is it even possible without otherwise compromising your health or well-being? Acknowledge your obligations, your job, your creative life, the family you wish to nurture.

Move in ways you enjoy. Let your body express who you are and what is important to you. If you watch your body in action doing something you love and feel born to do, you can see how perfectly your body was designed to serve and function. I might look with disdain at the middle-age flab on my upper arms, but when I am dancing I see how the length and shape of my arms are made to cut through space and allow me to express myself in response to the music I hear. There are those of you with bodies built for strength, for endurance, for nurturing. Notice the ways your body does just what it is intended for.

Wear clothes that fit perfectly and reflect your spirit. Learn what styles are most flattering to your figure, and don't be afraid to experiment with the new shapes that come into fashion. If the stores overwhelm you and nothing seems to fit, seek out an expert for advice. There will be more on this important topic in future chapters.

Choose empowerment. Self-criticism comes and goes, but you can decide that you are unwilling to

Notice the ways your
body does just what it is
intended for.

have your power and confidence sucked away by negative thoughts.

Lastly, try a little tenderness. So, you don't like your ankles. How would you feel if your precious baby daughter inherited them? Wouldn't you just want to kiss 'em? Be aware of your self-talk around your children and other young women. If someone pays you a compliment and tells you something about your body that they find to be beautiful, don't mentally disagree. Let it in.

Try This: Get Some Perspective

1. If a specific part of your body is really bothering you, try this exercise to help you get some perspective. Imagine a movie camera is focusing on the part of your body you are unhappy with. See the camera pull back, farther and farther away, until you are looking at yourself from a distance. Without the distortion and magnification that your displeasure creates, try to notice how this perceived flaw fits into your overall visual design. Can you see it as part of the greater whole? Is there something about it you actually like, or at least respect? Is it here for a reason, a result of a choice you made? Can you identify why you are leaving well enough alone, or why you aren't pressuring yourself into changing?

2. If you are nearsighted, try looking at yourself in a full-length mirror with your glasses on, and then take them off. Your reflection will look different when you are unable to see the specific definition you are used to focusing on.

3. Imagine the mail has just arrived, and in the stack is the latest issue of *Sports Illustrated*. You groan inwardly when you realize it's the swimsuit issue. But wait! The model on the cover has a body nearly identical to yours! Imagine how you would feel about your body if suddenly you were the latest and greatest thing. Try this idea on. At first it might make you smile or even laugh, but see if you can get used to it. Or mock-up your own magazine cover. Put a picture of YOU front and center.

becoming ageless

When I walked into her shop, the young woman behind the counter smiled and said to me, "I love your hair. It reminds me of Atlantis."

Atlantis, the legendary undersea world? I didn't know exactly what her reference meant, but it invoked an image of a mythological land of gods and goddesses, where beauty and harmony reigned.

My silvery hair suddenly felt light and luminous. What a gift her words were to me in that moment. Instead of the more typical compliment, "You look good for your age," this young woman gave me a window into what was beautiful and meaningful to her.

Every day is an opportunity to step into a new experience of yourself. Freely sharing an idea of beauty, one generation to the next, touched me. And it gave me hope.

growing more beautiful as you grow older

CAPTURING THE MOMENT

En plein air, the French expression for painting out-of-doors, is about seizing the moment, capturing the atmosphere and feel of the wind on the flat plane of the canvas. Painting quickly, the artist must describe the scene before the sun shifts. The color of the leaves, the curve of the river, and the light on the hills will never be just that way again.

Occasionally I do justice to the moment in time, the marks of my pastels creating a landscape as luminous and pleasing to me as light pouring through a stained glass window.

More often than not, my critical eyes focus on areas that don't communicate. Looking at the painting in my studio, I might decide to work on it further, only to find after hours of struggle that the painting may look different but it is rarely improved. Unless I can fix the problem with a couple of quick, deft strokes, I'm learning that it is best to leave the painting alone, to let it be an expression of the day.

How lovely it would be if we could *learn to see* ourselves like a painting of a beautiful landscape. Experience has taught me that any time I change the essence of a painting, something precious is lost. For the same reason, the value of plastic surgery is a source of debate. People who undergo this type of surgery often look different, but do they look better? Even when visible signs of aging have been erased, they don't necessarily look younger. They just look different.

LOOKING GOOD AT ANY AGE

"I'm afraid of all of it, of wrinkles and sagging skin, declining hormones, loss of memory. My identity is tied up with my attractiveness, and I'm afraid I am going to lose it. It is freaking me out!" Kim, 47

"I actually think it is easier to love ourselves as we get older, there is more of US, less of what we think we should be." Jane, 56

"For me, turning sixty is like taking the dark shadow of a mask off my face and letting my true light shine through." Jerie, 60

"I've always been introverted and unsure of myself. Now I have emerged from my cocoon. For the first time, I am comfortable in my own skin. I'm sixty-one, and this is the sexiest I have ever felt." Marianne, 61

"I feel good about myself. Someone tells me every single week I am attractive. The struggles in my life and the resulting introspection have made me a stronger person. I know who I am. I know my strengths and shortcomings. I'm not afraid to reveal myself." Carole, 67

As we grow older, our relationship to our appearance becomes both more challenging and more interesting. Our choices become more pronounced. Being aware of the passage of time heightens our relationship to the present.

Taking time to care for your appearance, and feeling pleased with the results, is important at any age. If caring for your appearance means striving to attain perfection, you will find growing older unbearably difficult and painful. There is nothing you can do to stop the aging process. Struggling to hang onto a youthful look has more to do with the past than the present. Again, you need to ask yourself, "What is authentically beautiful to me? What do I value? What is a realistic use of my time and resources?"

Here is the first step: Strike from your vocabulary these sentences: "You look good *for your age*." Or, "I look good *for my age*." You look good, period. That's it: No age qualifiers. Free yourself from the idea that you are a certain age with certain expectations and restrictions. If you don't feel you look your best, what do you want to do differently? I think it is the ultimate compliment to look at someone and have no idea how old they are. They don't necessarily look young, but they embody that certain glow and energetic presence.

No doubt about it, growing older can be a challenge, a cruel form of abuse to our already sensitive egos. Whatever birthday you most recently celebrated, don't let the conversation with yourself or others get too negative. Make a few jokes with your friends about the absurdity of what is happening and then continue on with your pursuit of looking and feeling fabulous.

I was too unsure of myself to be audacious and confident in my twenties, but I am making up for it now. My inner babe is alive and kicking, and I am taking advantage of it by enjoying my mid-life sexiness. I don't squelch my impulses or let opportunities pass me by. It helps that my profession keeps me tuned into the latest styles, and I never think of myself as too old to consider trying something new. *Bazaar Magazine* always has a section on how to wear the newest styles depending on your personal decade, but I ignore it. If I like it, and it looks good on me, I go for it, appropriate decade be damned.

"When I read the decade section in Bazaar, *sometimes the one that appeals to me most is the one for women in their seventies."* Lea, 40

Look around you. Incredible-looking women in their forties, fifties, sixties, seventies and beyond are everywhere. If you are still a youngster, my advice is to make the most of what you have right now, today. Enjoy this phase of your life to the fullest. If you take care of your appearance as best you can at every age, it is that much easier to move into the next phase of your beauty as you grow older.

THE CHANGING SILHOUETTE

Leslie and I have been inseparable best friends since we were fourteen years old. In high school she was the cute little blonde, and I was the busty brunette with the wild hair that I focused all my energy on trying to tame.

We raised each other and grew into adulthood side by side, celebrating our twenty-first, thirtieth, fourtieth and fiftieth birthdays together. I was there when she had her kids and buried her parents. When Leslie was forty-five, she was diagnosed with breast cancer. When our fiftieth birthday arrived, it was more than just the entry into a new decade: The real celebration was Leslie reaching the important fifth year of being cancer free.

Cancer treatments, while life saving, can come with a high beauty price tag. Chemotherapy put Leslie into instant menopause, and the estrogen suppressant drugs she must continue to take have had an effect on her body.

Leslie is thriving and looks great. But early and sudden menopause has changed her figure. "I'm at least fifteen pounds heavier and I have no waist! I don't like it, but what can I do?" she told me. "It is frustrating to have this shape and not know how to dress around it."

Over the past five years, whenever we've spent long weekends together shopping has always been involved. I've done what I could to find her cute outfits and bolster her confidence. Recently she was ready for a more comprehensive makeover. "Fly down here and clean out my closet," she said. "I can't stand this anymore. I look at outfits and remember what a good time I had in them, and even though I know they don't fit anymore, I can't get rid of them."

The morning after I arrived, still in our pajamas, we went to work. Trying on clothes that no longer fit isn't much fun, and in no time we had a huge pile to be given away. Clearly, the process upset Leslie. I knew that when she found more flattering options to replace the ones she had just tossed she would feel better, but that moment was still some time off in the future. "I knew my shape had changed, but I was horrified when we tried on all those old jeans and each pair made my stomach more noticeable than the last."

Always protective of my best friend, I was sorry she was so uncomfortable. Over lunch I tried every

Leslie is thriving and looks great. But early and sudden menopause has changed her figure.

reassuring platitude I could think of, but she wasn't buying it.

It was 4 P.M. by the time we arrived at the local mall, and immediately the shopping goddesses were with us. The new tops had structure through the shoulders and bust and were looser around her waist to just skim her middle. We easily found pants that fit her perfectly. "Once you showed me how to focus on my upper body and shapely butt, it was all good," she said.

As our bodies mature, shape and fit becomes even more important. Just when women need to see themselves clearly, they often turn away from the mirror, afraid to look closely for fear of seeing something they won't like. *Leaning to see* what is flattering on you at mid-life will help you step into your hard-earned maturity. Or show off your new found immaturity!

FADING FROM VIEW

The complaint I hear most often from mid-life women is that they feel drab, dumpy, out of touch. "I feel like when I look in the magazines, all the fashions are only appropriate for my college-age daughters," Judy, a longtime client, said recently. "I feel lost, like I have no style, like I can't relate to anything."

Judy needed to readjust her perspective. I assigned her homework before our next appointment. "Buy a selection of fashion magazines," I said, "and start cutting out everything that appeals to you. Don't judge how it would look on you, just look for images that you like." I encouraged her to look at the youthful layouts again with an eye for anything she could relate to, be it a color, an attitude or a creative combination. I reminded her that ads for accessories such as purses, shoes and jewelry always have a unique flair. For the moment, Judy's task was to concentrate on translating the looks of the very young into something that her ageless spirit could connect to.

On our next shopping trip, Judy expressed her pleasure with what we found:

"*These new shapes are fun and youthful, but the fabrics are more me, sumptuous and with an interesting mix of color and texture. I love the duffle coat, the bronze parka, the stretch corduroy jeans and cashmere hoodies in those rich browns and greens. My daughter coveted my big boldly striped sweater, so I let her borrow it. She wore it belted with jeans.*" You too can *learn to see* with fresh eyes instead of dismissing current fashion as something for someone younger, thinner or richer than you.

CONFIDENCE IN YOUR CHOICES

When I was in my thirties, I thought the early gray salting of my dark hair was a novelty.

Now in my fifties and mostly silver, I have mixed feelings about it. The questions for all of us, regardless of our age are "What are my options, and what are the best choices for me?"

To color or not color your hair as it begins to gray is one of many decisions for you to consider as you choose the ways to care for your appearance that are right for you.

At the moment, I don't color my hair for a variety of reasons. I've certainly had plenty of time to get used to my silver "highlights." I watched my beloved father's black hair turn to silver before he was forty. Since he was and still is a handsome guy, I never associated anything negative with it. I once asked Dad how he felt about his premature gray hair. "I didn't mind it until I was old enough to have it," he said. Since I have reached the point where my hair is no longer a novelty, I know how he feels.

I wouldn't choose to be prematurely gray, but I don't find it unflattering. I am conscious of making the most of it with the colors of my clothing, my make-up and my jewelry. I experiment with cool, edgy haircuts that show off the unique texture of my hair. I can't turn back the clock and recreate my rich natural hair color, with its variation of steely darks and warm chocolate browns, for any sustained length of time, no matter how skilled the colorist. It just isn't possible. What looks good the day it is colored is not so wonderful in only a couple of weeks, given the dreaded appearance of roots. When I consider coloring it every three weeks, I'm afraid that over time my coarse and curly hair would take on the appearance of rusted steel wool. My choice is to go with today's natural salt and pepper color, both because I believe it is more flattering, and also because it is more unique and interesting than flat, solid color.

Despite all my positive feelings about it, gray hair is not for sissies. I cringe whenever I see a photograph of myself shot using a flash, my hair glowing as stark a white as the moon. Many people assume I am older than I am, and I bristle if automatically given a senior discount. When I get over feeling paranoid about it, I can honestly say that the compliments far outnumber the mistaken senior identity. Women of all ages stop to compliment and question me, and men seem to not notice it and otherwise like what they see.

It all comes down to choices, and for the moment I am satisfied with mine. I consider that letting the natural graying of my hair take its course is not a default but a carefully considered decision. Sure, it takes confidence to let yourself be seen. Even though I am basically comfortable with my choice to have gray hair, I have moments when I decide I can't live with it another second. Even though I tell myself I feel drab or don't like being mistaken for a senior, the real reason is that *I am tired of needing the courage to be different*. Whenever I have these kinds of doubts, I say to myself, "No problem. If you want to change the color of your hair, do it, make an appointment with Jimmy. Go get those low lights (dark streaks) you have been thinking about. Or go a rich auburn. But let's just wait a week or two."

So far, the urge has always passed. I recognize that the doubt I feel is usually about something else, some other insecurity. For this insight, I credit the authors of *When Women Stop Hating Their Bodies*, (Random House, 1995) by Jane Hirschmann and Carol Munter. In their book they state, "A fat thought is never about your body." They explain that whatever uncomfortable feelings you are experiencing, you are quick to transfer them to the more familiar "bad body fever" with its refrain of, "I'm fat." Your negative refrain is whatever you think of as your BIG problem, from flab to wrinkles. One minute you are okay with who you are, the next minute you're not.

Confidence in your choices can wax and wane. If yesterday you felt fine about your exercise routine of biking and walking, and today you feel guilty about not going to the gym more often, something might have triggered that "not doing enough" feeling.

If the urge to color my hair lasts more than a couple of weeks, I trust that I will know that I have genuinely changed my mind, and I will go for it. So far I have been able to tell the difference between a choice that is an authentic expression of who I am and times when my inner critic has stirred up my insecurities.

Whatever choices you make, not everyone in your life is going to understand and get behind you. Not everyone is going to understand you, or for that matter, even *see* you. You're gorgeous to some, invisible to others. If you think back, it has always been like that. The popular girls in high school were either leggy blondes or perfectly pert little brunettes. Haven't you always felt that the beauty flavor of the moment was something other than you? Isn't it interesting that we all feel that way? Still, we are attracted to others and they are attracted to us. We find each other. Being true to your choices will help like-spirited people find you that much more easily.

"I've always felt good about my silver hair, I can see the way it casts a soft light around my face is flattering. Then I started internet dating. All the men dismiss me because I am too old. I hate it. But what am I going to do, color it just to make myself more appealing to all these guys looking for younger women? I just can't do it." Ellen, 54

"I don't have much gray, but I decided I wanted something bolder and more exciting, so now I color my light brown hair a deep, rich, spicy brown." Jane, 55

"I'm naturally a brunette, but at this time in my life being a blond works better for me. And my husband loves it." Jesse, 58

"Me? Go Gray? Never!" Vivian, 89

IT'S NEVER TOO EARLY OR TOO LATE

One thing is certain: It's never too late in life to *Grow* even *More Beautiful*.

When Kay called me to schedule an appointment to get her colors done and go on a shopping trip she said, *"I want to do this before I die."* At seventy-one, vibrant, energetic Kay did not seem in danger of dying anytime soon, but clearly she had waited long enough.

The colors that appeared in her palette were sumptuously beautiful, the textures of the fabrics luxurious and elegant. With a touch of lip and eye-liner, her soft features appeared in striking relief. Suddenly we could see that she had beautiful full lips, something neither of us had noticed.

On our shopping trip, Kay's beauty came alive. Warm peach and rose tones made her skin glow and subtle combinations of gray-green and smoky amethyst made her look refined and strong. The "big butt" she had warned me about was a total misconception, and once out of the baggy clothes she was wearing and into the proper size, she was transformed into a woman with a tall, striking silhouette.

Later Kay called to tell me, *"I am getting constant compliments. Everyone is just astonished. My sister-in-law didn't recognize me when she came to get me at the airport."*

It was true, Kay looked noticeably different. When I asked what took her so long, she said: *"My mother never paid attention to her looks or to mine. My husband didn't really care how I looked. It was never a priority for me until now."*

I'm glad Kay finally brought forth the beauty that had been always been hers to enhance. Taking care of yourself in this way fulfills a longing to be all you can be.

Don't wait. Women of all ages need support, encouragement, and advice to become all they can be. My client Julie, 39, perceptively put it this way:

"I find many women today in my age bracket (thirty to forty-five years) are simply overloaded. We are moms of young children, wives to tired husbands; and at the same time, we're in critical places in our professional careers. Many of us take on too much, and have a hard time saying no. We never learned to put our own needs first. Trying to find clothes that look good on our ever-changing bodies (often with our small children in tow) is about as easy as trying to change a flat tire in the dark when it's raining. Suddenly, you realize you are unhappy and you wonder why. So, if you can allow yourself the guilty pleasure of getting your colors done and having some fun finding clothes that look great on you, you just might remember what it feels like to be happier. It isn't selfish, it's putting the oxygen mask on yourself before assisting others. I still have too much on my plate, and I still worry about my career choices, but at least I don't worry about how I look in my clothes anymore! I am perfectly happy leaving that to a pro."

Start a section in your journal called THE TIME IS NOW.

1. Ask yourself the following questions: Is there something in the beauty realm you have always wanted to try but never have? What is holding you back?

2. Notice other women whose appearance you admire. Make a note in your journal and describe what intrigues you.

Start a list:

⊙ I notice…

⊙ I admire…

⊙ I'm intrigued by…

Is it the colors or clothes they are wearing, their self assurance, their comfort in their own skin? Maybe they look rebellious, age defying, athletic or strong. Do they remind you of yourself in some way?

Something you would like to become? Or are they a mirror opposite you can appreciate?

3. Appreciate the beauty of women of all ages, from the coltish teen to the elegant doyenne. While you can't turn the clock forward or back, there might be something about them that speaks to you. Perhaps you can recapture something you missed or aspire to something you feel drawn to.

4. No question about it, growing older helps you clarify what you believe in. The first summer you don your typical shorts or sleeveless top and are shocked by the sags and sun damage, you must decide if you are going to continue to be comfortable or start covering up. I had a "well-meaning" friend tell me my chest was too sun damaged to wear low tops. Even though what she said might be true, I'm not ready for high necklines all the time.

Start a list:

⊙ I feel self-conscious about…

⊙ My choice in response to that is…

Whatever your choice, honor your decision and the fact that you didn't allow yourself to be pressured into making it.

"My mother-in-law has looked superbly dressed for the thirty years I have known her. She will not wear anything she does not feel super in and I can tell that by looking at her! All this time I have wanted to emulate her, but I have never had the clothes knowledge like she has. But I am learning." Joan, 59

"I have a long face, a big nose and lots of wrinkles, but still people tell me I look beautiful, that I am radiant." LOIS, 77

Part Two   EXPLORE

becoming colorful

SPRING   Painting amid a field of blooming lavender, the hours deliriously pass; the hot sun causes long rivulets of sweat to meander down my back and between my breasts. As I try to capture the pure purple hue of this fragrant herb, I feel the color seeping into my pores, slowly turning my cells from whatever color they were before to this same shade of heady lavender blue.

SUMMER   The lakes in the Canadian Rockies are a shade of aqua that can not be described. There is a scientific explanation based on the reaction of the sunlight with the finely ground glacial particles suspended in the water. All I know is that as I walk the shoreline transfixed by the color of the water, I feel myself dissolving, turning into particles of the most luminous turquoise blueness.

AUTUMN   In the fall, nature offers painters the excuse to be outrageous. The late afternoon sun lights up the glimmering golden leaves, the red pepper trees cast long purple shadows on the dusty ground. I carry my paints and easel in the car in case I can't drive past a flaming vineyard without stopping and trying to capture it.

WINTER   Terry and I step out of San Francisco's de Young museum into the dusky winter twilight. After immersing ourselves in the experience of looking at paintings for the last couple of hours, our senses are saturated. Outside the museum the sun is setting, the western sky aglow behind the silhouette of eucalyptus and cypress trees. The evening air has faded to a burnished gold, much the same as the dim, slanted light favored by the painters in the 1890s. I feel as if I am walking into one of the fine paintings I have just finished viewing.

Chapter Three
color

✕✕✕✕✕✕✕✕✕✕✕✕✕✕✕✕✕✕✕✕✕✕✕✕✕✕✕✕✕✕✕✕

EXPERIENCE YOURSELF IN COLOR

"My colors are like the light of early morning, a time of mystery." Baunnie, *Clothe Your Spirit* workshop participant

Color is my second language. When I closely study my clients, their coloring speaks volumes, telling me stories of who they are and where they have come from. When I look at their colors, I see entire worlds, oceans, mountains, wildflowers, ancient rock-filled deserts, storms of passion, the strength of their characters, their warmth and compassion. I see in the mirror of their color palette all that they are and all that they are capable of becoming. Their beauty and originality shine like a beacon.

Even if you don't have access to a professional color consultant, or the idea of getting your colors "done" does not seem appealing, you can still engage in a dynamic relationship with color. Experience color in every way possible. Fill your life with color and colorful activities, and spend time indulging in the pure pleasure of looking at the color that surrounds you. Tune your eye and your responses. The more you look, the more you see.

The joys that color brings to your life, to your sense of your uniqueness and beauty, are almost too numerous to describe. Color brings moments of pure pleasure to your existence. It makes you feel vibrant and alive, nourishes and sustains you, and has potential to bring you into better harmony and balance. Can you feel the longing for more color that already exists inside you? Open yourself up to it. There are so many ways to bring the experience into your life. Learning to see and relate to color is like developing any relationship that is furthered by awareness. It takes time, practice, commitment.

Experiencing yourself in color is the heart and soul of *Growing More Beautiful*. The miracle of color is your ability to not only think about how it looks, but to sense how it makes you feel. Opening up to the sensation of color allows you to experience your uniqueness more fully. The *Growing More Beautiful* process offers a bridge from your enjoyment

Color brings moments of pure pleasure to your existence.

When the trees begin to blossom in late February, I start craving pink, pink and more pink: blossom pink, hot pink, raspberry and strawberry pink.

of color to showing you ways you can enhance your appearance by experiencing yourself as part of nature's color scheme. You can also use this knowledge and awareness of color to successfully build your wardrobe.

The more you interact with color, and the more you open up your senses, the more your ability to distinguish the subtleties in color grows. The more you look, the more your eyes *learn to see*. An obvious way to interact with color is when making clothing choices. You were created the same way as the world around you, and developing a physical sense of being "in color" enhances your experience of yourself and ultimately your experience of being beautiful.

When the ocean is a certain shade of blue-green, I'm struck by how similar in color it is to my eyes. When the sun breaks through an overcast sky and casts diamonds of light on the shimmering gray water, I am moved by the moment of beauty. Within the dancing sparks of light, I see a color not unlike the sparkling threads of my own silver hair. I may love the sight of all roses in a garden, but my heart opens to the crimson red bloom. Aquamarine, sparkling silver and crimson are all contained in my coloring, so I am attuned to them in ways that are different from the other millions of colors my eye is constantly taking in. Colors that touch my heart and spirit and enhance my appearance are what I call "resonant" colors.

Resonance is literally "an increase in sound by one body caused by sound waves of another vibrating body." It is also defined as being "intensified

and enriched." When I see a color that is in my own personal coloring, I feel a unique sensation, something akin to love or deep recognition. This is not to say I respond only to colors that are in my personal palette. I may react with giddy pleasure to radiant yellow blooms, especially against a vivid blue sky, but the feeling of resonance is a softer, deeper sensation, like a vibrational hum inside my body. Seeing my pearly pink twilight colors arouse a tender feeling in my heart, while the exhilaration of looking at the deep turquoise of a Caribbean sea makes me want to open my arms and soar into the sky. The particular emotional response, be it a sharp, sudden intake of breath or a softening of all the senses, is another way to describe resonance.

The sweetness of relating to your own special hues in such an immediate and personal way expands the concept of beauty. When you see something beautiful that moves you, it is like holding up a looking glass and seeing an aspect of your own beauty reflected there. Connecting with the world around you expands your sense of self. Fill yourself with that connection as a way to *Grow More Beautiful*.

As we move through life in harmony with the changing seasons, we have an opportunity to feel and express different aspects of ourselves. Winter pulls us inward, while we burst forth in time with spring's renewal. We crave wearing different colors every season. In the fall the reds of my sweaters and blouses begin to deepen from their bright summer hues, going from fresh cherry to deep cranberry and finally to rarest ruby by the time of the winter solstice. When the trees begin to blossom in late February, I start craving pink, pink and more pink: blossom pink, hot pink, raspberry and strawberry pink. My mood changes, and so does my lipstick. I also want a variety of richly colored clothing enabling me to reflect subtler shifts, expressing my energy on a daily basis. All of this attention to the colors in my wardrobe allows me to feel a greater connection to my inner self and the world around me.

At times, a longing for a color can come out of nowhere, and have nothing to do with what works with your coloring or your wardrobe. You just crave a specific color. Don't shy away, honor the craving instead. The benefits of certain colors go beyond what we wear, and may in some way be healing to your spirit. Surround yourself with that color in every way possible. Carry a swatch of fabric in your pocket and attach another piece to your refrigerator. Satisfy your hunger for that color with some thirsty new towels. Pick up a bolt of fabric or a garment in a color that grabs you and find your way to a mirror. Watch what happens. Don't be afraid to try something new, or question why some colors work together while others don't. Trust yourself to know if it is appropriate to add it to your wardrobe or not.

Growing More Beautiful isn't about restriction, only awareness. How we perceive color is in relationship to the color next to it. Scrutinize magazine layouts and furniture store arrangements. Compare the colors outside your window to the current fashions in department stores. If you are intrigued, check out a book or a class on color theory. It will change your life!

As you begin interacting more and more with color, watch for subtle changes to your appearance. I recently ran into Elisabeth at a party, and right away I could see something had changed. In the ten years I had known her, she had never looked so alive. "My knitting has gone from a hobby to a pastime to now one of the most important things in my life," she told me. "I love spending time in yarn stores, surrounded by all that color." It showed! For nothing is more beautiful than a person expressing themselves and radiating a love of life. Let color take you there.

USING COLOR TO BUILD YOUR WARDROBE

"Getting my colors done has been kind of like being able to carry around an honest girlfriend (with good taste) in my purse." Julie

Wearing colors that enhance your beauty communicates self-confidence. People unconsciously know you have a keen awareness about yourself. Wearing the right color is empowering, and it is sexy. The colors you wear introduce you to others. Having confidence in your color choices allow you to mix and match with ease, turning your clothing ensembles into works of art.

I recently did a color analysis for a striking African American woman with a thirty-year career in corporate fashion and cosmetics. She told me that when she worked at Calvin Klein in New York, employees were only allowed to wear black and white and only white flowers were permitted on their desks. A gift of red roses would need to be taken home. Now having relocated to the Bay Area, she was looking for new employment.

As I was doing her palette, I could imagine her in an outfit that reflected her energy. The fabric swatch that enhanced her skin tone was a pale bronze hinting at pink. I could envision it against a background of espresso brown, accented with cinnabar red. As she interviewed for a new position, those who met her would have more of a sense of her uniqueness than if she were dressed all in black.

Professional color analysis is a direct way for you to learn what colors and textures flatter and enhance your coloring and complexion. Through education and study, a color expert has learned to see color in a highly developed way. It isn't possible to explain exactly how to expertly assess your own colors, but I can walk you through what I look for as I create a color palette. With practice, and keen observation, you can learn to see what colors are most attractive on you.

First of all, what constitutes a flattering color? When I hold up a swatch to your face, I am looking for the color to heighten and brighten your coloring. I want to see your skin looking clear and smooth with a natural blush glowing in your cheeks. I want to see your eyes sparkle, their color enhanced. The color of your hair should harmonize as it forms a pleasing frame around your face.

Unflattering colors have the opposite effect. They bring out the imperfections in the skin, including dark circles, blemishes, lines and ruddiness, and they can make your skin look pale, sallow, yellowish, green, dull or blotchy. An unflattering color can literally look sour. Scary!

Before you worry that you are unknowingly turning yourself into a Halloween monster, rest assured that you will unconsciously avoid the colors that look the worst on you. You aren't attracted to them. When I was a kid in the 1960s and earth tones were "in," my parents suggested I buy new bedroom furniture in avocado and walnut. What? No way was I giving up my beloved bright pink in favor of colors I didn't even want to look at.

Knowing what color or "hue" you like is fairly straightforward. I don't feel good surrounded by earth tones like camel and rust, and they look terrible on me, turning my olive skin an unpleasant jaundiced yellow. Purple is a hue I love and feel good wearing. But what shade of purple is going to be the most flattering?

Purples reminiscent of eggplant, blooming iris and concord grapes are my favorites. Not every hue of purple works on me. The pinkish-purple that looks so pretty on candied eggs nestled with yellow chicks in an Easter basket is not a flattering color on me. Forget lilac, mauve or fuchsia.

Once I've determined a hue, there are other qualities I need to consider. I want the purple I wear to "hum" with my skin tone, eyes and hair. When a color "hums" it doesn't slide away, dull and unnoticed, but it also doesn't jump out at you and hit you over the head. If my favorite purple hue is mixed with white or gray, the color will fade to a chalky lavender that looks drab on me. If I mix it with black it will still hum against my strong coloring. If the color is "intensified" to the point of becoming a brilliant, electric purple, then people will notice the blast of color before they see me.

In addition to the word "hum," another term color professionals use to describe a flattering color is the term "kind." For example, off-white with a touch of yellow or pink might be "kinder" against your skin than a pure, unadulterated refrigerator white. Navy softens the hard edge of black, and dark chocolate looks richer and is often kinder than black. A kind color supports you, encouraging you to put your best foot forward.

A color palette contains a wide selection of hues of varying intensities. The most important part of the palette is selecting the most flattering shade of red. Red doesn't have to scream fire engine; your "best" red can be a *warm* red like salmon, persimmon or russet, or a *cool* red with a touch of blue like rose, crimson, ruby or burgundy cherry. Your best red isn't one hue, but a family of colors, ranging from light to dark. A light red can be juicy peach, sweet cotton candy or the soft terra cotta of weathered brick.

Your eye color provides the next clue as to a range of

flattering colors you can wear. If you have blue eyes, you can wear many varieties of blue, usually ranging from slate to navy to clear shades of blue that darken to cobalt. The same holds true for green eyes. A green-eyed beauty has interesting tones ranging from sage to moss to forest to emerald. Brown eyes often have rich greens in them, or gleaming golden lights that extend into all kinds of lovely warm tones.

The combination of an individual's best red with her eye color is always gorgeous. Imagine a dark-haired man in olive and port wine, a fair-skinned blonde in aqua and apricot, or an ashy brunette in sea green and English rose. Every person loves the moment when they first see their eye colors beside their reds because they can immediately sense the resonance that signals, "These colors are MINE."

After the range of reds and eye colors has been determined, I move on to select the other colors in the palette. Neutral colors, such as shades of navy, black, brown, gray and white are next. Your eye color will determine some of your neutral colors, and your hair color will determine them even further. For example, neutrals for auburn hair include glints of copper and rust; blondes usually have golden beige and butter cream; brunettes have a corresponding range of

Purples reminiscent of eggplant, blooming iris and concord grapes are my favorites.

browns; and silver heads get to play with gray and charcoal.

Due to their subtleties, neutrals are not as straightforward. It isn't difficult to decide if you favor orange over pink, but tan over taupe is trickier. It may take a bit of trial and error to tune your eye to recognize all the neutrals that look the best on you.

UNDERSTANDING NEUTRALS - HAVING FUN WITH COLOR THEORY

Neutrals are the backbone of your wardrobe, the structure that holds your ensembles in place. In paintings and in clothing, neutrals serve as the backdrop for their more stellar cousins. We don't necessarily want to wear all bright colors and walk around looking like a rainbow. There is nothing negative about neutral colors; the mixture of colors that create them makes them rich and interesting. They look beautiful worn alone and chic when mixed together. It is worthwhile to understand more about them. For that, we need a refresher in the basics of mixing color.

For most of us, our informal color education ended in elementary school. Some of us may have gone on to master organic chemistry in college but never learned something as useful and informative as color theory.

Let's start at the beginning. The primary colors are red, blue and yellow, and they combine to make the secondary colors: green, purple and orange. Blue, green and purple are cool colors, while red, yellow and orange are considered warm.

Let's look at the qualities in the fashion colors we call "neutrals." If you have ever worn navy, which is basically blue mixed with black, you know how frustrating it is to get different shades of navy to match. Navy can be a jaunty nautical blue, or it can have a dusty purplish cast reminiscent of blueberries. Soon you can start to see there is no such thing as a neutral that goes with everything. Gray (black and white) can be mixed with the primary colors blue or yellow, to make blue-gray or yellow gray. Secondary colors like green and purple can make a greenish gray or purplish gray. The other light neutrals like beige, taupe and camel are just as complex, combining white with yellow and tiny amounts of green, red and blue. These complex neutrals can be frustrating to match exactly, but they are interesting and expressive when combined with each other or with other colors.

Brown is the most complex and interesting of the neutrals and it is important to understand why. We've all tried to work with browns that don't match. My explanation of color fundamentals may help you understand and appreciate the potential of brown.

As a gleeful first grader playing with paint, you may have discovered that when you mix red and green you got a color that looked like mud. In other words, brown. Brown has endless variations. Add blue to the mix of red and green and you get a shade of brown that hints at plum. If you eliminate the blue and add more red, you get a different hue entirely, one more reminiscent of redwoods, cinnamon, or root beer. If you use more green than red you get a greenish brown, a deep olive color referred to as "breen." Mix in a dollop of yellow and your brown will turn golden.

Here's another consideration: How soft, bright or saturated any given color is depends on the intensity of the pigment, and whether white has been added to create a "tint" or black to create a "shade." When talking about the color of fabric, the dye and type of fabric is responsible for the final outcome of the color of the garment. If you wear black, I'm sure you've noticed

that not all blacks are created equal. Black velvet looks totally different than black linen. A napped fabric like velvet absorbs light rather than reflects it, making it appear deeper. You might find the way a certain fabric takes the dye makes the color more flattering on you. I can wear sheer white cotton but not white leather, shiny silver but not flat gray.

Most people who are unsure of their colors tend to play it safe, gravitating towards familiar colors. Black, also considered a neutral, is in a class by itself. The owner of a popular clothing store once remarked, "Customers come in and say they are sick of black. Then they invariably buy something black."

What is it about black? If you wear it, what do you like about it? If you wear a lot of it, do you ever get tired of it?

For all its popularity, black is not an easy color to wear. Only a small percentage of color palettes I do include black as a flattering option. It is hard to "glow" in black.

If it looks good on you, black has some great things going for it. It is subtle, both classic and edgy at the same time. Black feels sexy and solid, showing the outlines of clothing against skin in distinct relief. Nothing is quite like a black turtleneck, offering protection and minimizing exposure. Women who wear of lot of black tell me it simplifies their life because matching shoes or a jacket are never a problem. Plus, there is always a lot of it available, and often the coolest styles seem to be in black.

Even though it's in my palette, there are times when I just can't wear black. It feels demanding, harsh and enervating, totally out of tune with my surroundings. Other times the vibe is just right, especially with a piece of jewelry I want to focus on. Most landscape painters use black sparingly, if at all, because it isn't a color we often see in nature. We seek to bring light into our paintings, and black extinguishes light. Unless we want to create a somber mood or render a night sky, black is rarely used. Watercolorists don't usually use black paint from a tube, instead mixing it from specific shades of red, blue and green to give it more life. It can be convenient to wear black, but too much of it, too often, limits your opportunities for self-expression. You won't be as visible in it, and as a result, you won't connect with others as easily.

One of the misconceptions about black is that it "goes with everything." Black changes the energy of the color worn with it. If it is a bright color, black will intensify it. It can also cause the subtleties in a color to be lost or grow dull. I frequently hear, "I'll just wear that top or jacket with black pants," as if the pants won't be noticed. Women who know black isn't

the best color tell me they wear another color next to their face. It is always a good impulse to surround your face with a flattering color, but when others look at you they want to take in the whole of you.

We perceive color in relationship to the color next to it. When I'm doing a color palette, all the colors I select have a relationship to each other. They combine in a multitude of ways, and each combination is pleasing. Creating color "harmony" is as important as choosing any single individual color.

Imagine a man whose eyes and complexion were enhanced by olive green and wine red. The rest of his rich, saturated palette looks like the colors of an ancient Persian rug. Black looks great on him, but if he decided to wear clear sky blue it would be totally out of place with his other colors, even in small amounts. However, his tie could be a smoky blue, enriched with a drop of brown, the color of the late afternoon sky on a cloudless winter day.

"This morning, instead of coffee, I pulled out clothes and scarves and made a sort of mandala on my bed of colors and textures woven together. It was stunning and fed my soul. The rich greens and browns, the lively teals and dusty blue greens and cinnamons and raisins made a delectable feast for the eye." Jane

USING YOUR COLORS

You love color and are excited to go shopping. You head to the store hoping for sapphire blue to match your eyes and blush pink to flatter your complexion.

When you arrive you are greeted by acid green, mustard yellow and neon watermelon. You think to yourself, "Maybe I should just stick with black." Many manufacturers would love for you to permanently come to that conclusion, because it allows them to limit their risk by offering fewer choices. But women love color, and I hear from sales associates that a flattering garment in a "feel good" color is always snatched up right away.

All of your favorite colors won't be available all of the time but with patience they will eventually come into season. Fashion cycles bring in colors that are always a bit different than their predecessors. I had never worn brown, sticking primarily with charcoal and navy for my neutrals, until a few years ago when a rich raisin brown made an appearance. Now I love wearing certain shades of deep brown. It pays to stay open to something new instead of searching in vain for what has always worked for you in the past and being frustrated when you can't find it.

Color trends come and go. If your favorite red is this season's "it" color, then stock up on everything from polar fleece jackets to sandals. Different times of year showcase different colors, making some months better for finding your colors than others. In August, warm fall tones like russet and gold anticipate the colors of the upcoming season. By October, jewel-toned holiday colors are predominate. If you're longing for sapphire blue, try looking in November instead of March. March, the month of blossoming trees, is the perfect time to find the blush pink you are craving.

If you are uncertain about how a color is being affected by the lights in the store or in a fitting room, move closer to a window or ask if you can step outside to view your selection in natural light. If you are buying a navy print top in hopes that it will go with a navy skirt you have at home, be careful. You are right to be concerned if you are attempting to match a garment with one you have from a previous season. On the other hand, you don't always need to "match" your neutral colors. Look at the colors in nature for inspiration and think "harmony." Or add a third shade of navy that ties the two together.

What about a color you know is close but not exactly right, say the cotton khakis in that *slightly* off-green that fit too perfectly to leave behind? Try to get past your momentary lust for these pants and assess if they will harmonize with your other colors, or you will be fighting with them for their entire (short) life span in your closet. The other option is to buy a coordinating top at the same time, knowing that even if it, too, is slightly off, you will wear the outfit happily until you are tired of it. If you vary from your ideal colors, don't invest too much money, knowing it will get tossed soon after you have had your way with it.

The same technique applies to an "in" fashion color you are attracted to but can see isn't flattering. If you want to experiment with acid green, go ahead. A shot of it can look exciting with violet, chocolate brown and dark army green. Be playful. I went through a phase of being mesmerized by orange, even though it doesn't look good with my complexion. In

small amounts, with some judicious mixing with teal
or marine blue, I made it work. Not any orange would
do, either. It needed to be a hot, tropical mango that
stood up to my bold dramatics or looked succulent
with white. If you experiment with anything in the red
or orange family, don't neglect to adjust your lipstick.

A pattern or print that includes a color you don't
normally wear can also be a fun change as long as
the base color is flattering and the alternative color
doesn't dominate. When deciding about a pattern,
you need to consider your entire visual design, not

just your coloring. If your skin or hair has a lot of
texture, a fight may ensue. The shape and scale of
the pattern relative to your overall proportions is
important, too.

COLOR ANALYSIS

*"I use my color palette all the time. I love finding
something in one of my colors, but it also stops me
from making a bad purchase when the color just isn't
right."* Maggie

If you want to take greater advantage of the enhancing benefits of color to help you *Grow More Beautiful*, professional color analysis is an option to consider. With a palette of exquisite swatches at hand, you can make choices that allow you to dress in a more creative and artful way, trusting that the colors will guide you. Your personal palette narrows the search within the store, and helps you to build a coordinated wardrobe over time. The pair of shoes in an irresistible color will be guaranteed to work into your wardrobe, if they are part of your color swatch family. If you seek out colors that are just right, you will be rewarded with terrific freedom to be either boldly distinctive or softly soulful. The colors combine like a stunning painting or a haunting melody.

Beyond the obvious advantages of looking more attractive and shopping more successfully, it feels wonderful to be surrounded by colors you resonate with, that reflect your unique energy and essence. I have done hundreds of palettes, and no two are ever exactly alike; each is truly a unique "in color" fingerprint of an individual.

There are many misconceptions about color analysis, and I hope to address a few of them, as well as answer some of the frequently asked questions about using a color palette.

A BRIEF HISTORY OF SEASONAL COLOR ANALYSIS

The origins of professional color analysis begin in the 1940s, when the first form of individualized color analysis was developed by Suzanne Caygill. A training institute was formed, and the discipline of learning color analysis was then passed down through a rigorous program of study. One of the key ideas in this system held that a person's coloring naturally falls into a loose category that is reminiscent of a season of the year. The colors in a winter palette are cool, high contrast and intense; fall colors are rich and warm; spring colors are bright and fresh; and summer is like a shaded flower garden in July.

Then Carole Jackson published her book *Color Me Beautiful* in 1980. Jackson simplified, from an idea that was quite complex, the idea that personal coloring relates to a "season." When the popularity of color analysis exploded, largely due to Jackson's book, "schools" sprang up overnight, offering certification after only a weekend of training. To determine a "season," a set of fabric drapes were used and one of four coordinating color packets was dispensed. These quickie "palettes" were not individually done, and not only were these books of swatches incomplete, they were often incorrect. In the human population, there is a huge range of skin tones, eye colors and hair color. There is no such thing as a one-size-fits-all seasonal palette.

The other problem with simply categorizing someone as a "season" is that it is too easy to misinterpret. The most important criterion is determining if the skin tone is warm or cool. It is difficult for the untrained eye to guess correctly. Even I don't know by casually looking. I need the process of holding up hundreds of swatches to make a determination. Learning color analysis is demanding and difficult and today only serious lovers of color take on the challenge. If you have never had a color analysis done, and are interested in getting one, be sure to thoroughly research all the professionals you are considering. A well done color palette is a work of art, something you will enjoy for the rest of your life.

"The only way I can describe the experience of getting my colors done is that the sensation was similar to having my hair brushed. It felt so nurturing." Emily

FREQUENTLY ASKED QUESTIONS ABOUT COLOR ANALYSIS

How is a color palette different from colors I choose for myself by just looking?

In the wide world of colors, the majority of candidates for your color palette fall into the big amorphous cloud that is the "okay" group in the middle. The colors that are outside this group fall into two smaller groups.

In one group, the colors are pretty grim, either the wrong hue or intensity. They look muddy instead of clear, harsh when you need softness.

In the other small group are your very best colors. Not only do these colors look gorgeous on you, they harmonize perfectly with each other. When you choose your own colors, if you do so carefully, you will probably do just fine. With keen observation, you will be able to see the difference between colors that are flattering and colors that are not, thus avoiding the "grim" and pulling from the big middle. The real difference is that getting a color palette done by a professional will give you access to the best colors where the magic happens.

What will my color palette look like?

Preparation for creating the palette begins long before the client arrives. The fabric swatches used to create a palette are maintained with meticulous attention to detail, with variations in colors so minute that the untrained eye would be unable to distinguish the subtle differences.

A color professional chooses fabric swatches in a wide variety of textures and hues, from the most neutral to the most dramatic. The swatches are then assembled into a portable packet or fan. Pertinent information about how to use the color swatches to build a complete wardrobe is usually included.

I don't want to be limited. Do I have to follow it exactly?

A palette is not meant to be unduly restrictive, but if you only follow it loosely you will be frustrated because the colors won't quite go together. You won't be able to get those subtle nuances in your color combinations, because so much depends on just the right hue and shade.

When you are shopping, you can open up your color palette or fan and check a questionable color with the entire palette. If it seems to harmonize with the color in question, then go ahead.

Some people shy away from using a color palette for fear that it will limit creativity instead of enhancing it. I haven't found this to be the case at all.

I don't know if my skin tone is warm or cool. Why is this so important?

When you know your skin tone you can accurately select your best red, not only for clothing but for make-up, including lipstick and blush. If you color your hair, it will also influence your color selection. Your skin also has an undertone, and here is where it gets tricky. Say, for example, you are a fair-skinned blond. If you have a warm undertone your skin will have a golden cast, you will wear peachy lipstick and blush, and honey blond highlights will look great. On the other hand, your skin may appear to have a slightly yellow cast but your undertone can still be cool. If that's the case, your blush and lipstick will need to be rose toned and your highlights more ashy. I know this sounds confusing, and that it is difficult to visualize, but you probably have a feeling about how warm or cool you are.

Wearing the right color is important at any age, but when you reach the stage in life when you are covering gray hair or graying naturally, understanding your skin tone and choosing accordingly is crucial. It can make the difference between looking washed out and drab and looking beautiful.

Do my colors change over the years?

The biggest impact on a color palette is a change in hair color. If your hair color slowly grays over the years, the changes are subtle. If you start to color your hair, and the change from your natural color is dramatic, your palette will need to be updated. The good news is, you can adjust the palette to take advantage of your new hair color.

"I was originally a brunette, but after my hair turned prematurely gray, I decided to see if blondes have more fun. Jennifer has adjusted my colors over the years as I went from gray to honey blonde to platinum. I no longer wear gray, and overall my colors are brighter. My red is still rosy, but it is punchier. I just love it!" Laura

Hair color is an obvious change, but there are other interesting factors responsible for changes in a palette. I have done palettes for identical twins, and they have slightly different color palettes based on health and life experience. Colors often become more vibrant if an individual's health significantly improves. Anything that enhances a more vital life force, including creating art, enhances your ability to wear more color.

What if I don't like my colors?

In my experience this rarely happens because everyone usually loves their colors right away. But it is a good question. If you don't like your colors it might be because they are different than what you expected and may take some time to get used to. Unfortunately, it is also possible they are incorrect. No matter what, don't wear colors you don't like.

How can I prevent that from happening? Is your industry regulated?

Just as you would research any professional, ask about training and credentials. If you are uncertain, ask for referrals and to see examples of completed color palettes. Be sure to ask if each palette is individually done. There are certification programs, but no outside regulating body. The students I train now are several generations removed from the original creators. We all have a slightly different sensibility and point of view, which explains the variation between the results of different color experts.

Can I use my palette for interior decorating?

A color palette is an invaluable tool for use in choosing interior paint and home furnishings, helping to create a sense of comfort and pleasure in your living environment. Often people are better at choosing colors for their home interiors then they are for their clothing. When I do a color palette I often hear, "I have those colors in my home but never thought of wearing them." Surprise!

A color range we call the "skin tones" are soft, creamy colors enhanced with a touch of your red. They are lighter than your actual skin color so they enhance your complexion instead of matching it. You will look great in the light cast from interior walls painted in these colors. A color palette is handy when there is more than one person in a household. My husband and I both love red, and we use our palettes to collaborate on a hue we both feel comfortable living with.

I'm an artist. What is the value to me of having my colors done?

A color palette is a surprisingly useful tool for artists and painters. A painter needs to develop her unique color vocabulary, and a color palette is like an affirmation, a way to stay true to your individual sensibility. Most instructors favor a certain palette, and it is helpful to be clear and confident of your own color "home base," so you can learn from an instructor but not be unduly influenced.

1. Head to your closet. Don't worry about cleaning. Group all of your clothing together by color families. Put the browns together, the blues, the reds, greens, denim, black, white. Put your scarves on hangers according to color. Don't fuss about organizing, just enjoy the color. Hang them in your closet so you can see them. You can do the same thing with folded items in your drawers. Look over what you have.

2. Engage in some "Guerilla Painting." Do not try to create a major work of art. Grab a piece of paper from your printer; attach it to a clipboard or any stable surface. Find any kind of colored markers you have available: crayons, felt pens, colored pencils, whatever you can put your hands on in a hurry. Step outside and stop in front of the first colorful thing that catches your eye. Pick the colored marker that is closest to the color and scribble it on your paper or do a quick gesture drawing, the simpler the better. Move on or quit. There. This is how you start.

DRAWING AND PAINTING

A few words about drawing, sketching, scribbling and painting:

Make your mark – When you make a mark, a portal opens to you, transporting you to a different place. Making just one mark is an entrance into another universe. You stand before your paper and haven't made a mark, and then you have. That one mark links you to the experience of all other artists.

Let go of your aesthetic – You have an aesthetic that appreciates fine works of art and other beautiful objects. I know you are asking yourself, "Why would I make a mark that doesn't have meaning, that clutters up the world and isn't important?" You are allowed to do this for no other reason then you want a place to start. Directly engaging with color will lead you somewhere new.

Keep it simple – Always do the simplest thing you can think of so it won't seem like a chore or a duty. Start tiny! You can always graduate.

"I always think way too big. If I start something, I think it should be a masterpiece. I should paint a landscape or redesign my living room. I'm a single, working mother and most of the time I am too tired to get off the couch, but I also get depressed because I am not doing anything creative or anything that I love." Baunnie

painting a palette of words

How do you describe the aspens as they reach their peak of fall color beside a High Sierra lake? No words seem enough, because this shade of yellow orange is so brilliant, a gold so electrifying it almost doesn't make sense. The leaves seemed to shimmer with translucent radiance.

I am so excited by the color that I am breathless with anticipation to try and capture it in a painting. As I work at my easel, a couple stops by to check on my progress. "There is no way I could ever describe this color to anyone," one of them says.

My first painting of the trees reflected in the lake doesn't capture the intense experience of being there. I try again, focusing on just one tree against an azure sky. Better. As the sun begins to dip behind the peaks, there is time for one more try. Over a base of deep red violet, I blend brick red, clear orange, pure scarlet, warm and cool yellows, and touches of vivid green. As I work, the name of each color is like a flavor on my tongue.

Chapter Four
language

THE LANGUAGE OF COLOR

Color is perceived but language is known. At first blush we think of color as being purely experiential, but our connection to language makes the experience richer and more resonant. The names of things we love enhance our awareness, making our sensory recognition all the more vivid by engaging both sides of the brain. A word paints a picture in our mind, and giving names to colors brings us even closer to our experience of them.

When I do a color analysis for a client, the colors in the palette give me a deeper understanding of the person I am working with. I always take a moment to look over the gorgeous array of swatches on my desk and note which adjectives best describe the *quality* of the colors. Here are some of the terms I frequently use:

GLOWING	LUMINOUS	LIGHT	RADIANT
DARK	BURNISHED	STRONG	INTERESTING
COMPLEX	UNUSUAL	INTRIGUING	SURPRISING
WARM	EARTHY	RICH	BUTTERY
FRESH	CLEAR	CLEAN	DRAMATIC
STRIKING	VIBRANT	BOLD	SUBTLE
COOL	LIQUID	DEEP	

I'm not attempting to categorize the person sitting in front of me; I'm simply looking at their colors. Yet, my client always says the terms I choose seem to be describing them.

I like to see how the different aspects of the colors in the palette relate to each other. For this I use Yin and Yang, the easily recognized Taoist symbol of the interplay of forces in the universe. Yin is the dark element: passive, downward-seeking and corresponding to the night. Yang is the bright element: active, light, upward-seeking and corresponding to the daytime. Yin is often symbolized by water and earth, while yang is symbolized by fire and air.

A color palette always contains elements of both. Just as in nature, glowing and luminous are balanced by deep and earthy. Subtle and cool might share the circle with vibrant and strong.

Delicate brings to mind the lovely pastels of a twilight sky, and implies a light and tender touch.

THE LANGUAGE OF PERSONAL STYLE

My longtime friend and client Jane is a good example of seeming opposites coexisting happily together. She describes herself as *natural, refined, romantic* and *frisky*. *Natural* and *refined* seem like opposites but they are both part of her essence. She is as comfortable in an Alaskan bog as she is in a designer boutique. Jane has a voluptuous body, and her version of romantic is *goddess-like*. She goes through phases of loving anything cowgirl, and for fun creates stunning crowns and tiaras. Jane might wear a pair of perfectly fitted velvet pants with a down vest, and tie it together with a hand knit scarf and beautiful boots. She changes the buttons on things to make them more *playful* and *frisky.*

Using language is a way to connect with your uniqueness. We resonate with words and the images they create in much the same way we do with color. When you are looking at clothing and wondering, "Is this me?" there are many ways to use language to discover the answer.

Recognizing the multifaceted nature of who you are is the first step towards describing your individuality as it relates to personal style. My first book, *Clothe Your Spirit: Dressing for Self-Expression,* introduced the idea that we are complex, ever-changing individuals, not meant to fit into any one style category. At the time it was published, using categories to illustrate personal style was commonplace. Words like *sporty, natural, classic, romantic* and *dramatic* were popular. To me, those options seemed too limited. I was looking for something deeper, a richer way to connect to the essence of my clients.

SPIRIT TERMS

One of the most enduring aspects of *Clothe Your Spirit* is an exercise that helps you discover which adjectives best suit you. This process invites you to describe your physical attributes and inner characteristics, and put the two together to describe your spirit as it relates to clothing. The goal is to create a list of descriptive adjectives, and use them to guide you while you are making wardrobe decisions. It is one of the steps toward developing a unique personal style.

At any given moment, I am looking for words that express the different aspects of who I am. At this point in my life, I like the interrelationship of *sensuous, straightforward, fluid* and *sparkling*. These "Spirit Terms" describe both how I look and how I feel about myself, and they also apply to clothing styles. *Straightforward* and *sensuous* are strong terms; *fluid and sparkling* feel lighter. Without the light and dark, the subtle and the direct, the irreverent and the serious, I am not fully described. I am always seeking a deeper relationship with all aspects of my own inner duality, the yin and yang of who I am.

I also welcome opportunities to see myself a little differently. Each season, interesting new adjectives show up in the fashion media. This past holiday season I played with the idea of *edgy glamour*. Looking ahead to spring I might be feeling *playfully elegant* or perhaps *boldly refined*. I'll see what develops. At this moment I enjoy words like: *striking, undone, arty, easy, flirty, surprising, juicy, interesting, streamlined, bold, lush, wild, irreverent, relaxed and delicate.*

The last word on my list of current favorites is *delicate*, a term that stands out because it is different from its counterparts, a subtle bit of "yin." *Delicate* brings to mind the lovely pastels of a twilight sky, and implies a light and tender touch. I've never been attracted to *dainty, pixie* or other "small" words, but whenever I find myself attracted to an edge of ribbon or lace I notice how a touch of delicacy has found its way into my self-expression. Plus, what fun to put *bold* or *striking* or *wild* together with delicate and see what I can come up with. My Spirit Terms are my home base, but other words are places I enjoy visiting, my style vibe of the moment. Just like the role of orange in my color palette; not necessarily the most flattering when worn alone, but fun to fool around with.

Some great words I don't relate to personally are ones you might resonate with, such as *sporty, spunky, fresh, natural, classic, simple, clean, timeless, boyish, gypsy-like, playful, dramatic and sophisticated.* The Spirit Term exercise at the end of this chapter provides many more options.

There is a benefit to choosing Spirit Terms that goes beyond making choices about specific items of clothing. When women call to ask for my help, they often say they feel drab, lost, disconnected. Gaining weight in particular seems to extinguish the spark. I recently did a seminar for a firm that had quite a few plus-size women, and when asked to identify their Spirit Terms most seemed to draw a blank. They used the most tepid language to describe themselves: *casual, informal, natural, traditional.* There is nothing wrong with those particular terms, but together they aren't as engaging and vibrant as befitted this exciting group of women. With a little coaxing and the help of their coworkers, these initially reluctant participants were soon using much more dynamic words to describe their uniqueness.

Words that describe your essence help you stay tethered to your self-image even if the current fashion storm has blown right past you. The changing styles in clothing do seem to pass by in a blur, and it is easy to feel left behind. Spirit Terms are a way for you to hold onto yourself as you wend your way through life's changes and the craziness of fashion. You need to find the thread of who you are and a way to spin that thread into a rope you can use to anchor your unshakable sense of self.

The goal of choosing Spirit Terms is to develop a short list that you check in with when you are shopping, keeping you on track when deciding if a garment is right for you. Not everyone is attracted to describing themselves using language. Sometimes it is best to just let images come and not corral them with words.

"Knowing that my Spirit Terms are fun, snappy, feminine and direct really helps when I am shopping." Ellen

"I love the balance of flirty and fresh with deep, subtle and complex. I find that each term has a different kind of energy and power." Baunnie

"I use richly saturated and textured clothes, interesting beads and earrings, and suede cowboy hats to describe my rich, interesting, whimsical, gypsy-like spirit." Lois

THE SPIRIT TERM EXERCISE

I've included the complete Spirit Term exercise in the appendix that follow the conclusion of this book. This exercise is great to do with a partner or in a small group. It is fun to compare how your Spirit Terms are alike and how they differ.

FURTHER EXPLORATIONS:

○ **Sense of place**

A client searching for a Spirit Term that fit once asked me, *"Is there a word that describes Colorado?"* What describes you? For a fun twist on Spirit Terms, imagine your individual characteristics related to the qualities of "Place" such as cities, states, continents. Places that describe the way I feel about myself and the way I want to look include the hot, brilliant blue Caribbean; rugged, wide open British Columbia; arty Paris; sexy Rio de Janeiro. Other places clients have related to include: Australia, San Diego, San Francisco, Mendocino, Seattle, Boston, Hawaii, Santa Fe, Israel, New York, the Sierra Nevada, Bali, Provence, Barcelona, India, Los Angeles, Montana, Lake Louise, Arizona, England, Norway, Sweden, Botswana and Antarctica. The combinations are what really make it interesting!

○ **Color in nature**

Another way to use language is to list images you strongly identify with. My colleague Ronnie McCullough, owner of *Divine Color and Style,* has a special knack for describing herself and her clients. Once I asked her to tell me about images in nature that she resonated with. Here is her list:

"Still lakes, waterfalls, the sparkle of moonlight on snow, the pale turquoise of glacial waters, crystals, the reddest Chinese poppies, dragonflies, sea glass, the deep red orange of the flesh of persimmons, the color of Emerald Bay at Lake Tahoe, silvery green leaves blowing in the wind, tropical birds and flowers, lily ponds, leafless persimmon trees laden to bursting with their ornament-like fruit, magnolias, orchids, lemon quartz, the patterns of snowflakes. I like colors that have sheen, like the way rocks with metallic content sparkle and the way wet streets reflect – dark, but shiny with opalescent surfaces that change depending on the way you look at them."

What images in nature do you identify with? Make yourself a list, and add to it as you feel inspired. I found that I reread Ronnie's list many times and that it soothed me, the way a beautiful piece of music does. If someone else's words resonate with you, let them become part of your image vocabulary.

What are the adjectives that describe your favorite scenes in nature? Examples might be *calm, serene, peaceful, exuberant, gentle, dramatic, sparkling, rich and earthy.*

⊙ **Language in marketing**

Notice how clothing manufacturers try to intrigue consumers with visual adjectives. Here are a few of the names of colors I found in the 2007 Fall Patagonia Catalog. Some are obvious: *sea urchin, sable brown, mushroom brown, cayenne, Aegean sea, tinted ice, cranapple.*

Others make me wonder: *aurora borealis, afterglow, spark, hot ember, sprout, castaway, herbal tea, lunar eclipse* – part of the poetry and inventiveness of language. Watch for other vivid examples and notice what you are attracted to and how they make you feel.

My fellow artists were offering their critique of my work at the end of one of our painting session together. "Lush, dramatic, sensuous, rich," they commented. Even though they were commenting on my painting, it also felt as if they were describing my essence.

DON'T FORGET TO VISIT THE COMPLETE SPIRIT TERM EXERCISE IN THE APPENDIX.

lost and found

I am standing in front of a flower-laden arbor, totally at a loss as to how to paint it. The more I stare at it, trying to capture it on my sketch pad, the more elusive the simple form becomes. I am paralyzed with uncertainty, and don't know what to do to solve this puzzle.

With a sigh, I put down my pencil and sketch book and pick up my paint brush. Clearly I am not going to be able to capture this scene, so I might as well just play around with paint until this interminable painting session is over. Mixing up puddles of red, yellow and blue, I start painting the foliage around the structure. I figure even an incompetent painter like myself could manage to put in the sky. Soon I am lost in the patterns of light and dark, the sharp contrast in the foreground, the hazy colors of the distance. In a few more brushstrokes I've succeeded in painting around the elusive structure, and suddenly the arbor is in place.

understanding form

✧✧✧✧✧✧✧✧✧✧✧✧✧✧✧✧✧✧✧✧✧✧✧✧✧✧✧✧✧✧✧✧

FLATTER YOUR FABULOUS FIGURE

When an artist paints a figure, a portrait or a landscape, she is always studying relationships. Every object is in a relationship with what surrounds it. If the focus of a painting is a waterfall, it is the structure of rocks around it that define it. The same challenge applies to learning to choose clothing styles that flatter your figure.

Given the difficulty of seeing our bodies clearly, it is no wonder that we are magnetically attracted to style guides that tell us how to dress. Despite the many worthy attempts on the subject, my biggest objection is that no matter how many body types they use as examples, I can never find one that fully describes mine. Even if I could find a style guide that described me exactly, I wouldn't be in a hurry to peg myself as a certain "body type," especially if it meant I could only wear certain corresponding styles of clothing. I know you are dying to have the mystery of the perfect style for you revealed, but the good news is that if you learn to understand the nuances of your unique shape you can wear a variation on almost any style you like.

Approach the process of discovering what clothing styles look great on you with curiosity and an open mind. Developing a dynamic view of your body will help you take a flexible approach to the styles you can wear. When I am shopping for clients, the comment I hear most often in the fitting room is "I never would have thought of that." Women are so used to thinking of themselves in a certain way that they have trouble imagining anything different. Just like choosing black instead of color, when we are uncertain we gravitate to what is easy, safe and familiar.

In the chapter on Body Image I talked about how difficult it is to see yourself objectively, and in the section on Language I demonstrated how the qualities of your body are an expression of your spirit. The awareness you are developing about the unique aspects of your face and figure can be applied in choosing flattering clothing. With a little patient observation and a few practical tips, you can become

Developing a dynamic view of your body will help you take a flexible approach to the styles you can wear.

acquainted with your body and an expert at knowing what styles best suit it. Body consciousness adds another level of self-awareness that ultimately helps you radiate confidence.

THE SUBTLE NUANCES OF YOUR BODY

The challenge is in dealing with the ways our bodies have evolved and adapting to both our changing silhouettes and the changes in fashion. If we don't like our body, we keep having the feeling that it is our fault, that there is something we are supposed to be doing about it. Being in this mindset keeps us *looking but not really seeing.*

The most important goal is to understand your proportions in a loving but objective way. Imagine you are a painter doing a study of your figure. Think of all the minute dimensions you need to measure correctly to create your likeness. When a client and I go through her closet with an eye for proper fit, I learn the subtleties of her unique shape. After many years of working as a style consultant, I know what I am looking for. I pay close attention to specific areas by asking myself the following questions:

1. Are her shoulders wider or narrower than her hips?

2. Is her neck long, short, thin, wide?

3. What is the shape of her upper arms relative to her shoulders? Are they full, muscular or slender? Are her arms exceptionally long or short for her height?

4. Is her upper chest narrow or wide, fleshy or lean?

5. Is her upper and mid-back wide or narrow, especially relative to the size of her breasts?

6. Does her lower back narrow at her waist, or does it tend to be more full?

7. Does she carry extra weight above her waist in her midriff and mid-back, or below the belt in her tummy and lower back? Or both?

8. Does her waist curve in, out or follow a straight line? Is her waist high, meaning only inches below her breasts, or low and closer to the start of her hips?

9. Are her thighs slim, medium or heavy? What is their shape and tone? Are they fuller in the front, back or along the sides?

10. Is her butt narrow or wide, prominent or flat?

11. Does she have a long or short rise (a crotch to waist measurement) relative to her legs and torso?

12. What is the shape of her legs, including her calves and knees?

13. Are her ankles wide or narrow?

14. What is the size and shape of her feet?

I need to pay attention to the dimension of each curve in relationship to the overall structure of her body. It is especially important for me to notice how one shape flows into the shape next to it. For example, a woman who has narrow hips relative to a wider waist and fuller tummy is going to have a totally different silhouette than someone with slim hips on a lanky frame. If you were to ask yourself the above body nuance questions about your own figure you might not have a clear answer to each query; although I am sure you know the exact location of all your cellulite. Certainly it is hard to know if your

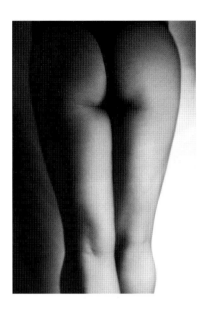

lower back is wide or narrow if you have nothing to compare it to. I don't expect you to be able to answer these questions about your own proportion as you read about them for the first time. If you want to understand the nuances of your shape, think of the questions as a guide to an ongoing investigation with a goal of learning more about yourself.

Remember that *learning to see* takes a fair amount of looking. In order to see, you have to be willing to look. The best way to educate yourself about your body is not to scrutinize it when you are just out of the shower. You've seen it (or not seen it!) all before and don't have the kind of objectivity you need for this kind of looking. Instead of *you* figuring out how to choose clothing, let's use clothing to help us figure out *you* and *the shape of your body.*

You can begin by learning from the clothing styles that fit you well. What is it that makes a certain garment so flattering? It might be the scooped neckline, the length of a skirt, or the way a pleated fabric shows off your shape but doesn't cling. When you discover something new that works for you, add it to your growing arsenal of flattering choices. There is also a wealth of information in the mistakes you excise from your closet. When you toss something because you never enjoyed wearing it, see if you can determine what was wrong with it. All the ill-fitting t-shirts with boring necklines also have sleeves that are probably too long and too wide. Learn from the misery of the loathsome low-rise pants that either slide too low or cause your belly to bulge when you tighten the belt that keeps them up. Swear you will never touch another unflattering crew neck, a jacket with droopy shoulders or a skirt with a funky hemline. See what you can learn so you can avoid the same unhappy mistake next time.

Fashion magazine layouts that feature real women instead of super thin models give you the opportunity to study how their bodies are similar to yours and how they differ. Now you can check out one of the many style guides for inspiration because you know you are looking to understand your unique shape better, not to follow their "body type prescription." You can also look at other women and what they are wearing in the same curious, open-minded way. We are ingrained to compare ourselves favorably or unfavorably, but if you can set aside your judgments you might actually learn something.

ASSETS AND FIT CHALLENGES

Although I see beauty and harmony in every figure, I am realistic when it comes to the challenge of finding clothes that fit. If everyone's clothes were custom made, there would be no such thing as a "fit challenge." If you were Empress of the Universe and all styles were created in your image, then everyone else would have the fit challenges because you would be the standard. Maybe in your next lifetime! For the moment, your body differs in a variety of ways from each manufacturer's fit model.

We all fantasize about clothes being custom created for us, especially when our fit challenges make a certain garment difficult to find. I had about given up on the low-rise jeans craze when suddenly The Gap introduced a shape called the "straight cut." For one bright and shining moment, I found low-rise jeans that fit me perfectly. Hallelujah! The same year they were discontinued because apparently there weren't enough of us non-curvy, straight-hipped types out there. I never found another pair that fit the same way, but did I blame my body, berating myself because my belly spilled over the top of any low jean tight enough to not slide off my hips? No, I did not. Instead I moved on to styles I liked better.

The secret to good style choices is learning to make the most of your assets. Focusing on camouflaging your perceived flaws only draws attention to them. Not only do you need to understand the structure of your body, you need to be its biggest champion and fan. If you can appreciate your unique body type, it will be much easier to clothe it successfully. If you can't quite get there, then act "as if" for the purpose of this learning process. If all else fails, pretend you are helping a friend. You want to learn how to choose styles that play up all of your womanly assets. If you are conscious of the lovely aspects of your face and figure, you will look for their beauty to be reflected back at you. When you see that the style isn't showing them off to their best advantage, from now on you'll pass.

Focus on the goal of highlighting your assets, and recognize there will always be fit challenges to resolve. Let me make one thing crystal clear: A fit challenge is not the opposite of an asset. No part of your body is inherently negative. In the right garment, like those straight cut jeans, my usual fit challenge turned my narrow hips into an asset. A fit challenge is simply that, a challenge.

If I have a thorough understanding of my client's assets and fit challenges, I don't need to figure out exactly what styles will look good on her in advance. I always make a list of my client's assets and challenges as part of our shopping preparation, but the styles I choose depend on all of my client's needs and desires, including her lifestyle, coloring and spirit. I consider what look we are trying to achieve and how I can use all elements, including style and fit, to accomplish this. I rarely say "No, that won't look good on your body type." Why not try it and find out?

Ellie is a curvy size 12 and stands just over 5 feet tall. When we went shopping, I found her a fabulous down vest in a refined fabric that suited both her spirit and her casual lakeside lifestyle. A down vest is normally the last thing you would think of for someone with a small frame and generous curves, but this vest was cleverly designed to create the illusion of a well-defined waist so it was totally flattering.

FOCUS THE EYE

Most women are so worried about their butt looking too big, or the roll around their middle, that they fail to pay attention to other equally important concerns. You need to direct the eye to all of your best features. If you ignore aspects of your body you are displeased with and hope everyone will too, you will look blurry and out of focus. You can't ignore a part of your body in hopes that it will just go away.

Imagine how a drawing of a nude figure would look if I left off the arms or smudged out the thighs. When you choose flattering styles, you need to consider all aspects of your body as part of the greater whole. Every outfit that shows off the figure to its best advantage is a result of all the pieces working together.

There are key assets on every woman's body. The following are a few tips on finding a garment that will bring out the best in them:

○ **Neck**

A flattering neckline draws attention to your face by highlighting the delicate balance between your jaw line, neck, shoulders, chest and bust. An interesting neckline can make an entire outfit sing. If you are seated, the neckline becomes the focus of your outfit. If your breasts are full, consider a deep V or scoop neck. A crew neck can make you look matronly. A blouse unbuttoned over a tank also creates an open neckline while providing more coverage. A small stand-up collar will elongate if your neck is short. Wearing a traditional button down is a personal style choice, but if you love the look of a classic white shirt, flip the collar up in back or leave it partially unbuttoned and let a lace camisole peek out. A lacy camisole also softens a deeply cut neckline, and can add a bit of color contrast. Save polos for sporty or athletic wear.

Just because some women feel bad about their neck as they age doesn't mean you have to. Don't hide in a turtleneck unless you are cold.

Instead, enjoy a variety of shaped and rolled collars and necklines. Add a fun scarf or muffler for layering warmth. Show off your striking collar bones and beautiful décolleté.

Shoulders

The shoulders of your garment define the structure of your silhouette. If they droop, you will too. Don't let big, structured shoulders envelop your frame. If your shoulders are slight, make sure the garment fits properly through this area. The fit of the armhole is important too. Broad shoulders welcome soft knits and suede instead of leather and other stiff fabrics that add bulk.

Bustline

The curve of the breast is a beautiful shape. Whether you are large or small, a properly fitted bra is a necessity. Smaller women who like to go braless still need to show some definition in order to give their overall shape balance. If your top is too tight, the eye will go right to the straining fabric instead of your beautiful curve. Pay attention to the shape of jackets, especially the lapels. A collarless or shawl

collared jacket or cardigan is a good choice if you are full busted, especially if you have small shoulders.

Midriff

The area just below your bust and above your waist is almost always an attractive curve. Don't neglect to show it off with proper attention to fit.

Waist

Even if you are heavy through the middle, you can create the illusion of a waist with the cut of your garment or a well placed belt. Experiment with a belt above and below your natural waistline. Always buy the size you feel comfortable in, but if a top that fits you through the middle is too big in the shoulders, then it doesn't fit. Same goes with pants. If they don't fit properly through the hips, move on.

Belly

There is no need to hide all evidence that you have a belly. Our culture has cultivated a lot of shame around this area, but you don't have to buy into it. A higher waistline in skirts and pants will shape, smooth and flatter. If you want to show off with a garment that sits

lower on your hips and draws attention to your belly, flat or otherwise, go for it. There are great fabrics that don't cling, but fit close enough to the body to show curves. Look for ruching, pleating or other gathered fabric that will skim over any fat you feel uncomfortable about.

⊙ Hips and butt
Show those curves! Take a good look at both the back and front view of jeans and fitted pants. The crotch should fit smoothly, not tug or bunch up into lines that resemble a "smile." There should be no extra fabric bagging under the bottom of the butt, or extra material to the sides of the hip curve. If the hips fit perfectly but the waist gaps (a common problem) have the waist taken in.

⊙ Arms
Sleeve length is everything. Women who complain about their arms change their tune when they try on a garment with a flattering sleeve. A short cap sleeve that flutters over the top of the shoulder is much more attractive than

one that cuts into the flesh of your upper arm. A ban on all boring square-sleeve t-shirts! A three-quarter or bracelet length is pretty; a camp shirt sleeve that hits mid-elbow is not. When choosing a dress, if you are self-conscious about showing your bare arms, look for a fitted sleeve in a sheer or light fabric. It helps to show the outline and shape of your arms as part of your overall silhouette.

⊙ Legs and thighs

Legs are a woman's glory, and a variety of skirt lengths can all be attractive, depending upon the shape of your gams. The same goes for shorts and cropped pants. Pay attention to the shape of the pant leg. The boot cut is popular for a reason; it creates a nice silhouette that enhances the curves of the upper body. There is no need to spend all summer sweating in long pants because you don't like your knees. As long as you don't draw the attention to them like a bull's-eye, no one is all that interested.

⊙ Ankles

If you have pretty feet and ankles, show them off. Make sure your hemline hits just the right spot on your leg to flatter. The shape of the shoe or boot makes a big difference, especially if there is an ankle strap. If you have thick ankles, ask for help finding a boot that fits.

As you consider all of the glories and challenges of finding clothes, you may wonder about using some of the shaping garments, such as Spanx, to smooth things out. Body shapers are gaining in popularity. It won't surprise you that I have an opinion about this. I cringed when I heard of something called "lipo in a box" that had a high-waisted style and was billed as a way to get rid of back fat. If they give you confidence and help you to feel sassy and sexy, fine. If you feel you *should* wear them because the world will be repulsed by your fleshiness, get over it. I hate to see anything become the next "should." Wearing a shaping garment under a clingy outfit for a special occasion where all eyes are upon you seems reasonable, but daily wear seems unnecessarily restrictive and uncomfortable.

BALANCED PROPORTIONS

It is not unusual for the widest part of your body to be one or two sizes larger then the smallest part. You are a woman and the fat has to go somewhere. It helps to learn the clothing manufacturers that have taken this into account and design for your body type. Note the size you wear in their clothing line.

Learn what styles will help you create balance and at the same time make the most of your curves. For specifics, see the style guide at the conclusion of this chapter.

When I said earlier that I had moved on from low-rise jeans, you might have been wondering where I went. Right around the time The Gap abandoned us straight hipped gals, I started noticing high-rise pants making a comeback. As soon as I saw a pair of wide legged jeans with a high waist shown in a Nordstrom catalog, I made a beeline for the store. Not only did I know the style would be more flattering because it would smooth my tummy, I knew the wide leg would help balance my fuller upper body. Styles come and go, but I know that the shape of wide leg pants, be it a flat front jean or a pleated slouchy trouser, is a good silhouette for me.

No matter how your body is shaped, you will want to wear an outfit with flattering proportions. You also will want to take advantage of something I call The Key Proportion. As a general rule, when laying out a painting, an artist is careful not to divide the canvas exactly in half because it creates an uninteresting or visually boring composition. The same general guideline holds true when looking at the proportions of an outfit. Don't let the garments that make up an outfit divide you in two.

The key proportion to remember is one-third/two-thirds. The proportion you do not want is half-and-half. Allowing your clothes to cut you in half makes you look short, chunky and awkward. Imagine a long blazer that hits you mid-thigh. The length of the blazer and the length of the remaining leg that shows will be exactly the same, half-and-half, 50/50. Now envision a shorter jacket, one that hits at the top of your hip bone. The jacket will cover one-third of your body, your legs will make up the other two thirds. Remembering the one-third/two-thirds proportion will help you look longer, curvier and more streamlined. To reverse the proportion with the longer length on the top, try a dress, coat or cardigan that hits around the knee covering two-thirds of your body while your legs from knee to ankle are the lower one-third.

Here is an excerpt of an e-mail I received recently:

"I've been thinking about you and thanking you for setting me on the road to smart shopping. You taught me a completely different view of my body – and I have passed it along to my daughters. Now when we go shopping we try on various items and we have honed our eye to the one-third/two-thirds view. Example: When my youngest daughter got married last month, I wanted a dress with a jacket. I found the dress, but the jacket was problematic. I finally found a beautiful jacket that was exactly right, but it was too long. So, I just shortened the length of the jacket and the sleeves. The shortened length made a huge difference and it looked fabulous." Karen

There are lots of exceptions to this rule, as the current layering craze can attest. Dressing in all one color lessens the impact of spatial divisions. One-third to two-third is the most elongating, but other proportion can be playful, like a short skirt or cropped pant with high boots. But if you are looking at yourself and you can't figure out why you feel squat and your overall look is clunky, check to see if you have visually divided yourself in half.

Wearing the correct size will aid you in creating a flattering proportion. If you are short-waisted or small-boned, experiment in the petite department, even if you are taller than the standard cutoff of 5 feet 4 inches. If the sleeves on a jacket are too long, check to see if it is available in the petite department. You might find that the garment fits better overall. If you have a long torso relative to the length of your legs, try petite pants. When shopping for jeans, try a longer length inseam in a jean that almost fits. You might need the length in the rise.

Experiment with trying on the same garment in a larger and smaller size. Clothes that are too big make you look bigger. Often, a smaller size will still be comfortable and will better show off your curves. Curves are supposed to show, not disappear. Skimpy is never flattering, and don't let your notion of a "number" prevent you from moving up a size or two if necessary. The combination of clingy and baggy is the worst. It will ruin your day unless you recognize it is the garment and not you. Also, be aware that clothes with a high percentage of lycra sometimes "grow" quickly out of shape. Even if you live for comfort, get the size that fits snugly instead of the one that is roomy.

Stand back and assess what you are wearing and how the garments form a silhouette that flatters your face and entire figure. I use the word and concept of *silhouette* even though it is synonymous with shape. When I paint, it is important that I step back and view my painting from a distance. Think of silhouette as your form outlined against a canvas backdrop. You can *learn to see* how the shape of your clothes are enhancing your overall body design. The form of your body is your ultimate asset, and you want to use clothing to highlight the overall structure as well as each individual curve and asset.

One final thought: Don't wear garments that are unflattering even if you think no one but the dog is looking. If your walking pants bag across your butt and you wear them all the time anyway, replace them with a pair that fits properly so you can admire your

nice booty on the way out the door. Lie around in well cut loungewear that makes you think, "Ooh, nice round belly," not "Ugh, fat stomach." Your clothes don't need to be baggy in order to be comfortable. Loving your body fosters respect and appreciation, which in turn alerts you to when you have found a garment that shows your body off to its best advantage.

"*Even though I am 5 feet 9 inches tall, my legs are relatively short, especially from the knee to the ankle. Regular length skirts make me look dowdy, but I have found that petite skirts make my legs appear longer.*" Yvonne

"*The difference between the 12R blazer and the 14P blazer was amazing. The waist of the 14P hit me in the right place, so suddenly my legs were longer and my waist shapelier.*" Donna

"*All my t-shirts were too big in the shoulders and too tight across my tummy. I started asking salespeople in a number of different stores for help, and finally found a few styles that fit beautifully. The spandex percentage seems to matter too. Up to three percent is fine but anything higher is too clingy. It makes a big difference in my overall look.*" Joey

"*I'm a pilates instructor, so my upper chest and arms are toned and well developed. I look for tops that are cut in a way to show that off, but also skim my waist and midsection where I am heavier. So long to ordinary clingy t-shirts that do nothing for me!*" Leslie

"*My thighs and legs are heavy, muscular and thick, but I have a long lean torso. I always start by searching for pants that fit perfectly, then on top I layer, play, play, play and have a blast. I'm tall too, so I can wear a short, full little dress over a jean or wide pant and still have the one-third/two-thirds proportion.*" Judy

FINDING GARMENTS THAT FIT

You will always be the last word on what you find comfortable and what you think is flattering. I find women are able to get in touch with their personal style more easily than they can figure out what size and shape fits them properly.

Just remember that styles constantly change, and something "of the moment" might be a perfect option for you. Unfortunately, old misinformation or a recent bad experience can blind you to what is really there, limiting your ability to choose flattering style options. It usually takes a recommendation from a professional to encourage you to experiment with something different.

Seek out people who can help you, and trust their advice. A fresh pair of eyes on someone blessed with talent and a positive attitude makes a huge difference. If you find a salesperson you feel comfortable with, come out of the fitting room and ask for help even if whatever you have on doesn't look good on you. The sales staff knows their merchandise and should have an idea of what will fit you better.

"I found a great sales person at J. Jill. She has real respect for breasts and bellies. She showed me how to layer a tank under a lightweight top for coverage that showed my curves. Her suggestions were so helpful." Jane

The key to finding clothes that fit well is patience. I know, it can be really hard and it isn't always much fun. It helps to know where to look. Just like knowing the colors that don't work for you allows you to eliminate them, it helps to know that certain manufacturers' styles will fit you well, and others' will not.

The following examples are department store lines, but the same holds true for smaller stores, boutiques and catalogs. Unfortunately, by the time this book is in print some of the above information will be out-of-date. Tried and true labels acquire new designers and change their silhouette.

MAJOR MANUFACTURERS – A STYLE GUIDE

- Lauren by Ralph Lauren, Jones New York and Liz Claiborne cut for a woman with a small waist and generous hips.

- DKNY, Calvin Klein, Kenneth Cole and Michael by Michael Kors favor women with wider waists and slim hips.
- BCBG, Theory, Laundry, Tahari and Max Studio are slim overall, especially through the torso and legs.
- Eileen Fisher flatters a wide variety of body types and is especially forgiving if you are a fit challenge. Her shapes tend toward boxy, so they don't work for everyone. But over the years her line has saved the day for me many times.
- The more expensive brands like Ellen Tracy, Anne Klein and Lafayette 148 are generously sized and tend to run larger. Some of the hip high-end designers like Nanette Lepore and Marc by Marc Jacobs are teeny-tiny.
- If you are larger then a size 16, but not quite large enough for plus sizes, you don't need me to tell you that your options are sorely limited. If you are short as well, finding clothes that fit can be a challenge. The size range starting at 12W and WP is more generous than traditional cuts, but smaller than a 1X. Eileen Fisher XL also helps fill in the gap.

1. If your curiosity is piqued and you want to consider the body nuance questions, put on your best bra and panties and spend a few moments looking in a full-length mirror. Choose a space in your home that is warm, well lit and where you won't be disturbed. Use a hand mirror for the back view. Don't spend too long at any one time. Just note what you see. If you catch yourself being critical and no longer gathering useful information, then stop and try again later. With a little practice, you will flip out of your critical mind set and start to notice specifics that will help you understand how you are actually shaped.

2. Divide your paper in two, and list your assets and fit challenges side by side. Add to the lists over time. On the following page note when something fits you well and explain why. Write down the styles you already know look good on you, but be ready to have that list change.

3. Start an I HATE THESE STYLES list. Put styles on it that you loathe. Baggy, clingy spandex t-shirts top my list; followed by super low, skinny, straight legged jeans; pointed lapels; and padded shoulders. Come home from a bad shopping day and call them names. Complain loudly about current fashion. Remind yourself that the style of clothing is the problem and not you.

4. What are the garments you struggle to find? What garments are always easy to fit? What might help you find what you are missing? You might be pleasantly surprised that when you clearly focus on the challenges instead of feeling vaguely bad about yourself, some of the unpleasant charge goes away. Always come back to asking how you can best support yourself.

Part Three   PREPARE

setting the stage

*L*ate spring on the California coast means a stiff breeze and an abundance of poppies, yellow lupine, and wild radish lavishly blooming in drifts of pale pinks and purples. On this May afternoon, the aquamarine sea is dotted with white caps. The sun is shining brightly as I set up my easel, but I know the moment is fleeting because the fog will soon roll in.

I long to plunge into my painting. My fingers itch to pick up one of my soft, brilliantly colored chalks. Pastel artists use the word "paint" to describe how they use their pastels. I calm myself, remembering that every successful painting begins with a strong composition. The colors of the flowers and brilliant water have caught my eye, but I need to consider the structure of the rolling dunes and the placement of the small, scruffy trees. If I concentrate on the principles of good design, the viewer will be that much more able to easily enter my landscape and share in the experience.

your lifestyle

TAKING A CLOSER LOOK

When I look into my client's closet for the first time, what hangs inside rarely matches up to how they tell me they spend their time. If they regularly go out to dinner, their cute summer dress is missing the coordinating sweater necessary to ward off the nighttime chill. Commuters who take public transportation never seem to have weatherproof walking shoes to take them from bus stop to office. I see stacks of turtlenecks and novelty sweaters, abundant collections of jeans, t-shirts and tank tops, but rarely the necessary pieces needed to create a complete wardrobe.

What do you need your clothes to do for you? To answer that question, you need to become aware of how you actually spend your time and honor what you need to be comfortable. It is one thing to love the latest "look" in fashion, another to have the pieces in

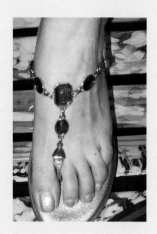

that "look" align with your lifestyle. Unless a garment is part of an outfit that meets your needs, you won't wear it. Your comfort needs not only determine the current usefulness of your wardrobe, they ultimately shape and define your personal style.

Take shoes, for instance. My active lifestyle demands comfortable shoes. No matter what is currently in style, I will not be wearing pointy-toed pumps or high heels. Unless my shoes fit perfectly, I'm unhappy. I insist that my shoes be flattering, attractive and well designed, and I never sacrifice practicality. When I give in to shoe temptation and the result is sore feet, neither the shoes nor the outfits that go with them ever get much wear. If I see that this season a slim pencil skirt will only look stylish with a high heel, I'll pass. Instead I'll choose a fluid, bias cut skirt that looks perfect with a pretty flat or ankle-wrap sandal.

"Some shoes I just can't resist. If I never wear them, I just make a little shoe shrine for them in my closet." Connie

No one likes clothes that don't breathe, are binding, tight, stiff, scratchy, or shoes that are downright uncomfortable. Beyond that, I see a lot of variation. Many of my clients love snug jeans and sexy shoes. Andy is unusually temperature sensitive. She gets easily chilled and easily overheated. Year round, every outfit she wears is multilayered. Nancy's skin is easily irritated by turtlenecks, wool, synthetics and cashmere. Tina needs year-round sun protection to prevent any further skin cancers. Yet temperature-sensitive Andy loves heels. We all have different tolerances and different priorities. When it comes to comfort, it is worthwhile to think through the realities of your lifestyle and determine what you need to be happy.

If you have lived in the same location for more than a year, you have a good idea of the seasonal temperature variations. The climate here in Northern California requires resourcefulness. The influence of the San Francisco Bay and the Pacific Ocean creates wide variations in temperature on a daily basis, with alternating microclimates of fog and sun. Today is March 11, and temperatures are in the eighties. Next week will probably be more typically overcast, chilly or windy here in Sonoma County. We can shiver during the summer and have a heat wave in October. We are only an hour away from the blistering heat of the inland valleys. Locals and visitors to our region need to be prepared. As we were discussing her spring/summer wardrobe, Janice said in frustration, "I can be going to church over in Oakland, and it can be cold and foggy and in the fifties, and then I'll go visit my family in the Central Valley and it might be in the hundreds." It is important that Janice know her requirements so she can create a wardrobe plan that meets her needs.

As you start to pay closer attention, you will notice the times you don't seem to have the right thing to wear. Learn to anticipate those needs and, when you are planning your wardrobe for the upcoming season, think ahead.

The first time I work with a new client, I ask them a seemingly endless list of questions about their lifestyle. Most people think of their lifestyle in very simple terms, usually work, time off and going out. In reality, the lives I hear about are much more complex and interesting. Andy describes herself as a "Playground Mom," but has other charitable and social obligations when she needs to dress with style and flair. Even life on the "playground" can be a challenge, beginning with school activities in the morning and Little League games in the hot (or cold and windy), late afternoon. "It drives me crazy to have to change clothes over the course of a day," Andy told me. "I want to just be able to add and subtract layers."

In preparation for our upcoming shopping trip, Julie, an Early Education specialist, wrote:

"I spend a lot of time with young children – mine and others – so it is important that things are easily cleaned. Dry cleaning isn't out of the question, but it isn't practical for my everyday wear. In my field people tend to dress casually, but since I'm in a manager role I need to dress professionally, yet not stuffy or corporate. I like the idea of being able to dress up an outfit so it might have two purposes. For example, if I work at my daughter's nursery school one morning and then go to a board meeting at night, it would be nice to not have to completely change, unless of course I'm covered in paint. I'd love to be able to just switch shoes, throw on a different jacket and a little lipstick. I often don't have any time to do much else! But if I'm going out for a social evening with "grown-ups" I want to look totally different; cute, sexy and fun."

Michelle is an architect who works from her home office. During the week she relies on easy care, business casual clothes, pulled together enough to meet informally with a client or contractor on short notice. She spends long hours at the computer, so everything must be soft and comfortable. When she tours job sites, a shoe with a rugged sole is essential. When she makes a presentation she needs the elegant look of fine quality professional wear that exemplifies her design aesthetic.

Michelle has found that the core of her wardrobe is nice looking casual clothes that also fit her needs on the weekends. *"I need to be careful not to spend my entire budget on those important professional pieces because they only account for 25% of my time. It is tempting because they are so beautiful, but I have to stay focused on finding wonderful things that I can wear everyday. In my case that means washable jeans and slacks, t-shirts, sweaters, light jackets, weatherproof outerwear and walking shoes. I'm a designer and I love color and texture and always want to dress with flair, even if I'm running to the post office."*

Here are some other priorities.

"It doesn't bother me to change multiple times during the day. In fact, I like changing when I get home from work, or putting on something festive to go out to dinner." Judy

"I'm a realtor, and outside of work I rarely dress up. I crave my athletic shoes. Most of my free time is spent with my dog who loves the water, so mud is usually involved. I'll wear something cute as long as it can easily be hosed off." Yvonne

Although we have four distinct seasons, I usually see my clients twice a year, combining two seasons and covering the upcoming six months. After we discuss day-to-day activities, I ask them to look ahead to include all upcoming special events. What will they need for the holidays this year? Are there occasions such as weddings or an important birthday coming up? I encourage them to get at least one outfit for all the delightful surprises sure to come their way, such as a party invitation, a gallery opening or a night at the theatre.

If you travel for business or pleasure, think of your needs throughout the year. It helps to keep a mental or physical list of what you need from season to season. If you regularly travel for recreation or to visit family or friends, what will the weather be like and what will you feel like wearing? Thinking of what you need for a quick weekend trip is a good framework to help you focus on what you need in your day-to-day life. If you can only take a couple of pairs of shoes and one jacket, what would they be? Planning ahead will make packing less of a chore.

We all seem to need those jackets and sweaters to leave in the car "just in case." Winter coats and parkas are never a problem for me, but for several years running, I noticed I never seemed to have the appropriate jacket to wear in the spring. Once the flowering trees start blooming, I shove my dark, heavy coats to the back of my closet. As the stores are filling up with summer merchandise, months of chilly weather are still ahead. I've started to collect pretty cardigans, mid-weight jackets, and protective rain gear in fresh spring colors whenever I can find them. When I layer them together, I can enjoy the morning sun and still be protected from the late afternoon gusty winds. Chilly Andy has learned that she can never find the heavier sweaters she needs during the summer in the stores at that time, so she is on the lookout for them year round. Don't make life more difficult for yourself by shopping for what you need at the wrong time of year. Buy bathing suits in the summer and parkas in the winter. Anticipate your needs, and shop when the stores have an abundance of merchandise.

Thinking of what you need for a quick weekend trip is a good framework to help you focus on what you need in your day-to-day life.

Think about the support structure of your wardrobe. If you are keeping a journal, dedicate a few pages to making notes on your clothing needs relative to your lifestyle. Another option is to create a computer file so you can easily refer back to it, update as needed, and e-mail to your stylist!

How will you spend your time in the months ahead? Jot down the type of clothes you need for each category. Make notes about specific requirements.

Step One - Assess your needs

1. Work:
   Everyday/office
   Meetings
   Special events

2. Time off:
   Everyday/daytime
   Everyday/evenings
   Social activities, special events
      and entertainment
   At home – Lounge and sleep wear
   Recreation – Sports and exercise wear
   Travel
   Formal wear and special occasions

Step Two - Clarify how you spend your time

Assigning percentages will help you see how you actually spend your time. Making a simple pie chart is a good idea too. This useful step will help you understand why you have gaps in your wardrobe.

Example: Here is how architect Michelle spends her time. Her needs during the work week are as follows:

- Everyday/office – 75% of work week

- Client meetings – 15% of work week (Refined professional dress with flair, evening and dinner meetings are more relaxed but also dressier.)

- Client presentation – 10% of work week (Professional wear that exemplifies her design aesthetic. Elegant, fine quality, coordinated outfits.)

- Weekends (Same as everyday/office wear but clothes should be suited for long walks and casual lunches out. Evening dinners and movies require a coordinating jacket.)

- Special occasions (Office holiday parties, formal home entertaining and weddings and graduations.)

a wealth of abundance

Having driven 800 miles in our motor home, we arrive in Mount Vernon, Washington, to shop at the Mecca for all pastel painters, Dakota Art pastels. I am nearly hyperventilating with excitement, and wonder if the three hours remaining before the store closes will be enough.

My shopping alternates between careful selection and utter abandon. I choose paper, iridescent pastels, sets of pastels that are on sale. The owner of Dakota points out a chalk color that can only be described as "neon shrimp." I can hardly wait to try it.

When I am finished shopping I crawl out of the store back into my RV, too tired to eat anything but cheese for dinner. Making a piece of toast or holding a fork would require too much effort.

It takes days to organize all my new materials when I return home. Some items are arranged in my studio, others fit into my outdoor painting set. We painters might look messy in our splattered togs, but we must know where everything is. You never know when the light will be just right, or a tree will have just burst into blossom.

I love abundance. I love to own lots of luscious things. But it is the awareness of what I own that makes me feel rich.

YOUR CLOSET AS A WORK OF ART

The state of your closet is a reflection of your sense of self and directly relates to your ability to put together an outfit that expresses and satisfies. No one's aiming for perfection, but consciousness is definitely required. You can't look and feel your best if your closet is disorganized, confusing, and out of step with your needs and lifestyle. Your closet is the place where you stay current with who you are. You want to see where you are so you can move forward.

Dozens of books and thousands of articles have been written about how to best get organized. Custom closet systems and organizers are big business. I'm not going to advise you how to best arrange your closet and your drawers; only inspire you to make the effort it takes to keep your wardrobe updated. Ongoing closet organization provides the backbone of *Growing More Beautiful*.

UPDATE AND ORGANIZE

Keeping your closet current and updated takes time. Ideally, a clean-out and reorganization should take place twice a year. Fall and spring are the transitional seasons that allow us time to prepare for the cold of winter and heat of summer, and are the ideal seasons for closet evaluation and organization. The weather during these transitional seasons is variable, in fall ranging from an Indian summer heat wave to the first major winter storm. In the spring the tease of early warmth gives way to biting wind late in the season. But variable does not mean unpredictable. The climate where you live might seem quirky and unusual at times, but year after year brings basically the same challenges.

I can help a client clean her closet in a matter of hours, but my semi-annual process of doing my own closet is accomplished over a period of weeks. I like the way the changing seasons motivate me to prepare for what is ahead. In August there is a quickening as all the fat fall fashion magazines start arriving, right around the time I am getting bored with white linen. My work as an image consultant requires that I jump into the fashion swing of things right away, and I need to be able to get dressed to shop for fall clothing in downtown San Francisco on the hot Tuesday after Labor Day. Time to jolt myself out of my laconic summer frame of mind and get organized! Once I've cleared out the clothes meant for mid-summer heat, I'll assess what is left that will take me through the next six weeks of early fall. It will still be warm midday, but mornings and evenings will be cooler. I perk right up at the idea of wearing richer colors, and I'm excited about the potential of some of the new fashion trends. By mid-October I've pulled my sweaters and heavier slacks out of storage, and begin to ready my closet for the first cold or rainy day.

As I pack away the last of my warm weather clothes, I take the time to do a final purge. Did I wear out or stain something that now needs to be tossed? More important, I need to make decisions about the garments I never wore at all. If during the course of the season I try on something a couple of times and then immediately take it off because I am not satisfied with it, I set it aside to be given away. Anything I haven't worn all season I know I will probably never wear again, and it goes into the giveaway pile too.

When you put away clothes until the next season, be sure to clean them thoroughly. Moths love to nibble on dirty woolens, and spots you can't see will be impossible to remove months from now. Plus, you can anticipate the pleasure of your clothes being fresh and ready-to-wear when you next need them.

Once the transition phase of Indian summer has passed, I am well on my way to converting my closet to support me during the months of cold ahead. All my open-toed shoes and summer purses go into storage, and my winter shoes and boots take center stage. At this point, I'm concerned with outfits. Do I have everything I need to feel complete? Is there something I wore regularly that is now tired and

Fall and spring are the transitional seasons that allow us time to prepare for the cold of winter and the heat of summer, and are the ideal seasons for closet evaluation and organization.

needs to be replaced? What new pieces would update what I currently own? What exactly am I missing? What am I craving? I can't answer these questions until I know what I have.

For this step I enlist the aid of my trusty collapsible rolling rack. A rolling rack functions as a mini second closet, and it is a great organizational tool for assisting you in getting items out of your closet, so you can assess the current status of your wardrobe. Everything I still love from last season I hang on the rack. The "maybes" stay in my closet for now, and I'll try them on as time permits, checking closely for fit and wear.

Meanwhile, I've probably done a wee bit of shopping for myself. My new purchases go straight to the rolling rack that I have been using for sorting. I hang last season's favorites beside them. Keeping everything in plain sight inspires me to play, creatively mixing and matching old and new. I anticipate what I want to wear over the holidays, and any special occasions or trips I have planned. As outfits are completed and I start wearing them, I put them into my closet. I've started an annual tradition of finishing my seasonal cleanout in time for Thanksgiving. Seeing my family gives me an incentive to set aside the best giveaway stuff for

Keeping everything in plain sight inspires me to play, creatively mixing and matching old and new.

them, and while I am at it, I finish the job and pack away clothes to be donated.

When I feel my winter wardrobe is more or less complete, usually in mid-November, everything is returned to my closet, and I fold up my rolling rack. I may still have a list of items

I want to look for, but I will be able to quickly dress in the morning for the busy day that lies ahead.

When spring is around the corner, start the process again. As the daffodils emerge, and flowering plum trees burst into blossom, get out your rolling rack. Put away your darkest velvets in favor of fresher colors. Spring is a transitional season like fall, where the sun can tease us one day then disappear for weeks. Keep your boots and woolens handy, but pull out a pair or two of sandals just in case. Catch the excitement in the air and look ahead to the pleasure of next season.

It would be ideal if you were able to leave your rack up for a period of weeks, but if space in your home is limited you can collapse your rack and put it away between organization sessions. Designate a section of your closet as "in progress" so you can easily pick up where you left off as time permits. Using the rack instead of laying garments on your bed allows you to clearly see what you have and makes sorting easier. Keeping clothes on hangers makes returning them to your closet easier, too. It is depressing to be running short on time and have

a big jumble of shoes and clothes strewn all over your bed! A freestanding rack is also an invaluable tool when you are deciding what to pack for a business trip or vacation. Leaving it standing in your laundry room where it can do double duty is a way to get it out of view but still have it handy. I swap out my dresser drawers each season too, storing my alternate season's folded clothing such as tank tops or sweaters in large, stackable bins. Having a couple of empty bins handy will help you tackle one drawer at a time.

TOO BIG, TOO SMALL OR
JUST PLAIN WRONG

What to do with clothes that no longer fit is an issue that needs to be addressed. In the "Body Image" section, Connie talked about how good it felt to clear out what no longer fit and make room for new things that did. But we didn't do a total purge. When we were cleaning her closet, we moved the items that were too small into the guest room closet. If after a couple of seasons the clothes still don't fit, it will be time for her to let them go. We only saved the most beautiful pieces, figuring we could replace the less expensive items such as t-shirts if she lost weight.

However tempting as it may be, there is no reason to save all of your too tight jeans, even if you plan to lose weight. Get yourself a pair that fit, and if you lose weight, buy yourself a smaller pair. Even if your old ones fit again, they won't look as good as you remember because jean styles change subtly every season. If you must, save your favorite pair or two, but not every single pair.

Even if size is not an issue, there is still plenty to be done. If you love clothes and shop regularly, you are going to end up with too much. Mistakes happen. Some items will be your favorites and some garments won't work out as well as you might have hoped. There is no reason to feel bad about your need to weed. Editing, learning, moving forward are all part of the creative process.

I have few qualms about giving garments away that I'm not wearing or enjoying. I feel guilty having clothes just hanging there when they could be back in circulation and of use to someone else. Plus, chaos makes me cranky. I love the feeling of abundance that comes from getting rid of distractions. I can't claim to always be tidy, but I am nourished and supported by the harmony of organization. Others have commented on the phenomenon of "less is more." If you weed out all the clutter, you can actually see what you have. Before a shopping trip, I always clean out someone's history of wardrobe mistakes. "What will I wear before our shopping day!" they wail. Later, they tell me that even though they felt like they had nothing left, they actually had more to wear.

My colleague Marsha Silberstein has enjoyed a long and illustrious career in fashion. She is fearless about mixing a twenty year old shoe with a contemporary outfit. I asked her how she decides what to keep and what to get rid of:

"*The first thing I look at is its lasting value. Is the item a classic, well made, timeless? Will it mix in with new looks and stay fresh or will it drag the overall impact down? The last thing to consider is its dollar value. Just because an item was expensive to buy does not necessarily make it an enduring style.*"

HELLO-O-O IN THERE

If you don't have the time or inclination to regularly clean and update your closet, you can still learn from its contents. If you are frustrated by "a closet full of clothes and nothing to wear," take a closer look whenever you have a free hour. We all tend to buy what is familiar and what fits easily. Everyone's closet seems to contain an abundance of one type of clothes, but a paucity of the items it takes to make a wardrobe work. Depending upon your body type and shopping preferences, some items are easier to find than others. When Sally first called me she said, "*I have dozens of black turtlenecks and nothing else, and I still buy more black turtlenecks!*" Are you someone with as many black pants as Sally has black turtlenecks?

Last week I went to help Joanne with her closet organization. We set out all her favorites on a rolling rack, and stood back to assess. Joanne had a fabulous collection of beautiful and unique jackets, several nice fitting pairs of slacks, and some great shoes. Unfortunately, she didn't have many outfits because she was missing tops: coordinating t-shirts, blouses, knit shells, or what are called the "underpinnings."

"It seems obvious now," Joanne said, "But sometimes you can just stare into the contents of your closet and not know what is missing. With my broad back and narrow shoulders, tops are a fit challenge for me," Joanne continued. "I avoid trying them on and gravitate towards the things that are exciting or I know will look good on me. I can see now I need to make a point of getting some underpinnings so I can wear the clothes I already own."

HELP IS ON THE WAY

It is important to set aside blocks of time you can devote to keeping your closet healthy and vital. If you know you will procrastinate or avoid doing the necessary weeding and organization, consider enlisting a buddy to help you. Offer to do the same for her. A closet cleaning and wardrobe assessment is also a great time to enlist professional assistance. An unbiased opinion of what to keep and what to get rid of can be invaluable, and a fashion professional can advise you on how to update the things you already own. A wardrobe evaluation should also take advantage of looking at your clothing to explain what styles and shapes will flatter your figure. It is an opportunity to discuss what pieces to add and where to go next, and to get acquainted with new fashion options. A wardrobe consultation is subtle and uniquely personal. I don't just clean closets. I evaluate a wardrobe with a deeper understanding of the individual's spirit that comes from becoming acquainted with their colors.

Find the way to update and maintain your closet that supports you and your desire to *Grow More Beautiful*. There is no right or wrong inside a person's closet, only the items that reflect their spirit at this moment in time. Let your closet be a reflection of your beauty. Creation is inspired by simplicity, not chaos and blind spots. Enjoy the treasures you have collected, and make them accessible so you can revel in the pleasure of adorning yourself. Take the time to make it happen.

"When I buy something new it always motivates me to get rid of some of the things I haven't been wearing." Lucia

"When I bring a new item home, I try it on right away with different pieces and I see what combinations I can create. Otherwise, I'll tend to wear the same outfit over and over, and I want a variety of looks from every garment." Daria

Enjoy the treasures you have collected, and make them accessible so you can revel in the pleasure of adorning yourself.

Try This: Assess Your Wardrobe

As you are going through your closet, make notes of what you are missing. The goal is to get a clear idea of the gaps in your wardrobe. You may want an entire new outfit for a neglected aspect of your lifestyle, or decide to focus on finding pieces to coordinate with garments you already own.

Step One – Identify when you have nothing to wear!

- Note the times in your life where you truly have nothing to wear. Do you avoid activities because of it?
- Consider all aspects of your lifestyle.
- Review your notes from the previous chapter.

Step Two – Where are the gaps?

- You have some great pieces but they aren't complete outfits. Be specific about what is needed so you can wear them.
- Note the *lone wolves*, items you love but you have no idea where they fit in.

Step Three – Add the finishing touches. What is needed to complete the look?

- Undergarments
- Hosiery
- Shoes
- Purse
- Belts
- Jewelry
- Other accessories

Tip: Write down everything as you go so you will remember what you need. Digital photographs are a handy reminder and can be stored on your computer. If you are on a roll mixing and matching, take a second to snap a photo to jog your memory. Or put your outfits together, including accessories, and leave them hanging on your rolling rack for a few days to give yourself a visual imprint.

planning your wardrobe

GETTING MORE OF WHAT YOU WANT IN YOUR LIFE

Now that you know what you have and what you need, take a moment to reflect on where you want to go.

As you move forward and begin thinking about the specifics of your clothing needs, you have an opportunity to use this process to help you *get more of what you want in your life*.

Your life is a reflection of everything you have put into it. Now is the time to ask yourself what you most long for. Looking ahead, is there something that would bring your life into better balance? How can the expression of your deepest desires move you forward in the months ahead?

After I consider my practical clothing needs, I always ask myself the question: "What do I want more of in my life?" The answer becomes the underlying theme in all my wardrobe decisions.

Think of all the challenges you have met in your lifetime. Raising children, saving to buy a house, dedicating yourself to helping others – all require sacrifices and trade-offs. Yes, it took effort, took you out of your comfort zone, and demanded a lot of you. But notice your courage, and how strong and determined you were when it came to meeting important goals, and all the amazing things you have accomplished.

More. You want more. Let the power of your intention weave its way into your everyday decisions.

Assume that the desire to look your best is a given. Connecting with your deeper needs will help you put all your decisions, from what to toss from your closet to what new clothes will replace them, in present time. Don't sell yourself short on this important tool for creating what you want.

The answer to what you are most hungry for can be as simple as a single word mantra:

- Freedom
- Flexibility
- Beauty
- Order
- Prosperity
- Comfort
- Time
- Visibility
- Play
- Romance
- Adventure

It can also be specific, like a relationship, a new job or a new living situation. What would help you attain that? Would dressing more professionally enhance your career? Do you need a confidence boost in order to project your attractiveness to the opposite sex? Be clear about your intentions and desires.

If connecting with others is one of your desires, it helps to think about who you want to attract. *In general,* men do not relate well to high fashion clothing. What is fresh and exciting to those of us who follow trends can look bizarre and silly to them. I've had my husband ask me with genuine puzzlement, "*What **is** that? A costume?*" If you want to be creative, save it for your women friends and other fashion followers who will appreciate the effort.

Men don't have their comparison radar out in the same way women do. They respond to warmth and a self-confidence that is inviting and not intimidating. They sense that a critical self-judge will also judge them harshly. Show them who you are and where to look by highlighting your assets.

More. You want more. Let the power of your intention weave its way into your everyday decisions.

your money

◇◇

"Help! I can't continue to make bad choices with what little money I have to spend on clothes." Julie

AFFORDING WHAT YOU LOVE

You are ready to head out the door with your list in hand and your mind percolating with ideas. Wait just a moment, there is still one more detail to clarify, and it is a big one.

Before I end a wardrobe evaluation session, there is a final consideration before we next meet in the fitting room. What is the budget? It is a hard question, but it is important to come to terms with how much you have available to spend on a shopping trip. Money is a loaded issue that stirs up feelings of deservedness and vulnerability.

Setting a budget helps to clarify where to shop and how to prioritize. If I don't have a specified amount for my client, I don't know where to begin. I need to know what type of store or department to shop in, and I also need to know the kinds of clothing that are the priority.

Think of a "budget" not as a harsh form of deprivation like a "diet," but as a guideline for healthy spending. It is not the dollar amount that is important, but the consciousness that you bring to it.

Keeping the focus on "wardrobe" is crucial. The advantages of shopping toward the goal of building a wonderful, working wardrobe seem obvious, but it is difficult for women. Many women find it easier to approach the task in a sidelong way instead of head on. They buy a t-shirt here, a pair of shoes there, without considering the entire picture. From a financial perspective, this can be costly. No one can afford unworn mistakes, or individual articles of clothing that don't make an outfit.

I have compassion for how difficult this is. Clothes should not cost as much as they do. The last time I was buying a car I was overwhelmed by how expensive all my choices were. I didn't know how to face such a big financial decision, and I found myself wishing I could just buy a piece at a time. Couldn't I just buy a steering wheel this month, a set of brakes the next month? Then I envisioned myself with my steering wheel and brakes in hand, not understanding how everyone else was driving around in fully assembled vehicles.

It would be a total waste of money to only buy parts of a car and still not have usable transportation, but that's how most of us approach our wardrobes. For a variety of reasons, including the expense, we don't face the issue of cost head on and instead buy bits and pieces of clothing. When it's time to get dressed to go somewhere, we are totally frustrated that nothing suitable goes together. We don't have a choice when buying a car, real estate or other large purchases. We have to determine the full amount we can spend so we have a place to begin our search. With clothing, our need to make financial decisions is ongoing. The more you can come to terms with what you have to spend the more successful and satisfied you will feel.

FINANCIAL CHALLENGES

I'll be outlining the specifics of "wardrobing" in the upcoming chapter on shopping. For now, let's look at your financial challenges and the approaches that will best support that.

- **In addition to money, the other resource there never seems to be enough of is time**.
  Many important things compete for our attention, leaving us short on time for shopping. If we had more time, we could spend some of it searching for bargains and discounts, and save money. If we had more time, we could search down the final item that would make an outfit complete.

Recognize and honor your time vs. money equation. This may mean shopping at large department stores or locations you know will have what you need in stock. It may mean you don't have time to pick through sales racks. Or it may mean that making time to find a bargain is worth it to you.

- **Be clear on what you expect to purchase for your money.**
  When a client gives me a budget to work with, I need to know what she expects for the money she has allotted. If the amount is not large enough for everything she hopes to buy, then we have to adjust accordingly.

- **Buy clothes that fit.**
  Buying clothes that fit properly is a true money-saving practice. If you own one pair of pants that fit perfectly, you won't need five that almost fit. If something almost fits, you have to juggle the rest of the outfit to make it look decent. When a key piece flatters, creating the rest of the outfit is easy.

- **Learn to prioritize.**
  It is fun to update your wardrobe with the new fashion trends, but no one needs to redo their wardrobe every season. This winter you might decide you need to update your coats and outerwear, and next year you realize your casual wear has been neglected for too long and needs attention. Decide what you are going to focus on each time you review your budget.

- **Set parameters for cost per item.**

  If a total budget figure seems overwhelming, then break down what you consider to be a reasonable cost per item. It will help you avoid spending too much on an item that isn't a high priority. I don't feel the need to spend a lot on jeans, casual clothes or handbags, but I will spend more on shoes and jackets. I am also thinking about cost per wear, and which pieces are pivotal to my lifestyle.

- **Tune in to what will satisfy you.**

  Even if a lack of money isn't an issue, more clothing isn't the answer. Too much gets in the way and requires additional time to deal with.

- **Be aware of the emotional challenges.**

  Even when you face up to the issue of money directly, there are still emotional land mines and pitfalls to be gently dealt with. Craving new clothing and compulsive or unconscious spending are not crimes. Many of us do it, myself included. Learn to honor your desires, and at the same time be aware when spending makes you feel worse instead of better. Remind yourself of all the things that are important to your spirit. Keep asking how you can best take care of yourself in an appropriate and satisfying way.

- **Negotiate with a partner.**

  Spouses may not understand or value your needs, and it can be a lot of work to come to an agreement about clothes spending. Difficult negotiations with a partner can bring up your own issues of deservedness. Ever snuck something home in the trunk of your car and waited until your spouse wasn't around to unload it? You are not alone! Just remember, you deserve to look fantastic and wear your clothes with pride. Chances are, your partner wants you to look good too.

- **Honor yourself.**

  Money may be tight in your household, and you might feel guilty placing your needs above the needs of your family. If you are overweight and feel guilty about it, and money is an issue as well, you are in a tough situation. All I can say is that many of my clients are women who ignored their own needs for so long, that when they finally tried to take care of themselves, they had no idea how to go about it.

- **Shop smart if time and money are both in short supply.**

  Set a modest budget (with realistically modest expectations) and schedule a twice yearly appointment with an in-house personal shopper. She will help your money go as far as possible. Ask for an appointment on one of the store's sale days. Another idea is ask your savvy bargain loving friends for help and suggestions. Most are flattered to have their skill acknowledged. Ask about stores with deep discounts, and see if they will take you to their favorite consignment or resale stores. Catalog retailers also offer discounts off-season. At the end of winter, for example, Lands End puts out a clearance catalog that offers fleece and down jackets at a fraction of the original price.

My favorite money-saving trick is this: If I don't need anything specific but crave a clothing treat, I limit myself to one thing that I can cut the tag off and wear immediately, on the spot, or at the latest the next day. It helps me to focus on finding something I need, and the immediate gratification does the trick. If I don't find anything perfect, I know I can always try again the next time the shopping bug bites.

Like all aspects of *Growing More Beautiful*, learning the most satisfying way to spend your money is a process. The more you practice, the better you get at making conscious supportive choices.

"The most difficult thing about my job is my customer's lack of knowledge about what clothing costs. They expect to get everything they want for an unrealistic amount of money." Lea Perez, Executive Personal Shopper, Macys by Appointment

I don't work outside the home, and I struggle with spending money on myself. It took me a long time to get up the courage to call you. When my husband first saw all the clothes he was shocked, but it helped him to see me as a person and recognize that I, too, have needs. Now he loves both the way I look and my improved self-esteem, and always encourages me to call you." Diana

"I regularly shop the department store sale racks, but I only buy something if I have something to go with it, or can find something just right at the same time. I've learned that odd pieces are no bargain." Daria

"I have heavy hips and thighs relative to my small torso, so pants are a fit challenge for me. I've learned that it is worth it to spend more and get a quality pair that fit perfectly, altering them if necessary. I can spend less on tees and tops, because they are an easy fit for me." Linda

"Once I realized I was wasting precious time feeling like I had nothing to wear, spending money on bad purchases, and feeling bad about the way I looked, I released myself from the notion that personal shoppers are only for ultra-rich women. I allowed myself to get my colors done and to go shopping with Jennifer. I was totally amazed by the transformation…just what the colors alone did to lift my spirits and energy. Then when my clothes actually fit, I felt ten pounds lighter and overall so much sexier. It's way easier to look good when you have a great selection in your closet to choose from. I'm saving time and money by knowing everything in my closet suits me!" Julie

Part Four   ENVISION

dreaming into reality

When I was house hunting several years ago, I was discouraged beyond description by the houses that were available in my price range. We had already sold our condo and needed to make a decision soon. In desperation, I decided to make a collage. I totally let loose and asked for what I wanted, fantasies beyond anything I thought I could afford. I picked colors I loved, and added rooms awash in sunlight and gardens filled with tropical flowers. Carefully, and with great discrimination, I attached it all to a board, including photographs of my husband, Katie the dog, our RV, even the Golden Gate Bridge so I would stay in range of San Francisco. The final thing I glued on were the words "A ceiling made of sky."

A few days later I found our house. It wasn't what I envisioned or what I thought I was looking for, but it had an incredible view, a true "ceiling made of sky." Looking at my collage later, I was amazed at how many elements of our new house had appeared on my collage. These special features never appeared on my practical list of what I was looking for based on what I thought I could afford. But there was my blue-green kitchen, my red bathroom and my ceiling made of sky.

images

CREATING A COLLAGE OF IMAGES

The next season in fashion is always on the horizon. Stores are constantly filling with fresh merchandise. At this point you need a tool for both clarifying what you are looking for and helping you find it. Fashion magazines and catalogs offer you all kinds of examples of current styles, from practical to the over-the-top fantastic. In some form or another, these are a sampling of the garments you will be choosing from. Instead of being overwhelmed with too many choices when you get to the stores, you can do some "advance shopping" from the comfort of your home.

To help you prepare, cut images you like from magazines and put them in a file or create a "look book" using a binder and plastic sleeves. Any editing you do beyond just tearing out images will help you further refine your choices. Assembling images by gluing them to a large piece of poster board, and creating an actual collage takes the process a step further.

It engages your senses to put your hands on something and interact with it. Rip, tear, cut, arrange, add, subtract, glue, tape, step back, put it up, look at it, let it in – these are all actions that will help you connect with clothing that expresses your spirit.

A collage of visual images is where practicality meets artistry, and fantasy turns into reality. In its simplest form, creating a collage is a tool to help you see what expressive clothing actually looks like. We don't want to just stay warm and dry, we want to be inspired! Creating a collage helps you envision what you might want before you see it available for purchase. It wakes up your eyes and your senses to the possibilities.

This deceptively simple tool yields powerful results. Over and over I find this process connects a woman to her essence and turns the concept of dressing for self-expression into a reality. Looking at magazines and catalogs is part of my wardrobe evaluation service, and the odd and unexpected images my clients are drawn to are the most revealing. We are not always conscious of what we like, least of all able to articulate it.

Creating a collage helps you envision what you might want before you see it available for purchase. It wakes up your eyes and your senses to the possibilities.

Dressing for self-expression is not static: You don't find a look and then stick to it. Not only do you evolve personally, but fashion is constantly evolving and changing. It is important to acquaint yourself with new style options, and magazines and catalogs are where you do your homework and find out what is available. The biggest challenge if you don't shop frequently is being able to relate to the current fashion in the stores. Looking at what is available helps the eye to adjust and make connections.

You don't need to analyze fashion unless it interests you, but you do need to learn how to react to it. Not every new trend will be right for you, but some of them will be. The way to know is to respond to what appeals to you. Open up a magazine or catalog, and mark or rip out everything that catches your eye. Don't let it get you down that you are not as thin, young and rich (or air brushed) as the models featured on the pages. What these celebrity icons look like is beside the point. You are connecting with the agelessness and utter fabulousness of your spirit. If you like something, some form of it will look awesome on you.

For the moment, don't concern yourself with being practical. If there is no place in your life for a fur shrug or you don't have the body type for skinny pants, it doesn't matter. If you like it, rip it out. Your instincts will ultimately guide you to focusing on styles that look good on you. If a particular look seems impractical but you love it, there is probably a variation that will be more wearable.

Shopping is filled with the practical realities of searching for sizes and comparing prices. Clothing stores can be overwhelming or not have what you want. No wonder you come home with another black turtleneck. Let your imagination pre-shop for you so you head to the stores inspired. I believe that doing collages brings the clothes magically into your life. If nothing else, preliminary preparation helps you keep your eyes open for just the right thing. When you find the perfect thing, you experience the pleasure of knowing it is right without the doubts.

Looking at magazines like *Lucky*, thumbing through catalogs like *Anthropologie*, and reading the "Style Watch" section of *People* helps me stay up to date and current. The looks that appeal to me might be geared to a woman younger than I am, but I want to keep that sense of attitude, of being hip and fresh. If the entire trend seems too young for me, I translate a part of it I like and adapt it to my look. A couple of seasons ago I saw actress Scarlet Johannson on the cover of *Bazaar* magazine in a sheer lavender dress, her eye make-up dark, her hair a messy tangle. I thought, "I love the way she looks, those full breasts, pillowy lips, the wild hair. I wish I could have been confident enough to be like that when I was her age."

Remembering back, when I was in my twenties smooth-haired Cheryl Tiegs and Christie Brinkley were the models to emulate. Wildness was not "in." I never considered playing up my voluptuous features and messy curls. I wanted to be pretty, to fit in. But why should now be too late?

I ripped off the cover of the magazine and put it in my pile of images to be made into a collage. The moment I was drawn to that image, I let myself "grow" into my wild, sexy, voluptuous potential, and over time I have integrated it into my style of visual self-expression. It is never too late, or too early, to be all that you are meant to be, to know and claim who that is. The magic of *Growing More Beautiful* is using time as your ally instead of your enemy.

"Instead of looking middle-aged and predictable, you keep me looking like a rock star! I love it." Donna

"Bazaar always does a section on what to wear depending upon your age. I often think what they show for the thirty year old would look better on the fifty year old. Why do they do that?" Ann

I consider my collages to be life-size interactive beauty affirmations. When I look at a finished one, I know that the woman who made this collage must be beautiful. I hang many of my clothing collages from past seasons up in my studio where I can look at them. I like being surrounded with images that reflect my spirit. People wander into my studio to look at my paintings and they often linger over my collages. I have been doing this practice for many years, and whenever I look at the collages I am amazed at how many of the clothes I actually own. It is a real-life manifestation of the power of intention.

Nothing could be simpler than creating a collage – no art skills are required! Magazines, scissors, poster board, a glue stick are all you need to get started. The trick is finding the time. Consider the process as nurturing time for yourself instead of one more thing on your long to-do list. Sometimes just connecting with the image is enough. I'll spend a Saturday morning in bed, shopping in magazines and catalogs like I was in a store with money to burn. It is so satisfying to connect with things in current fashion that I like and the images form the basis for my next collage. Who cares if I have nowhere to wear it? I can have all of the fun with none of the work. The amazing thing is, your spirit is satisfied whether you actually own it or not. This is especially supportive when your wants and needs exceed your financial circumstances. You can stay present with your spirit instead of getting caught up in the need to have more.

When I do a wardrobe consultation with a client I always create a quick collage on the spot. Some of the images selected surprise both of us. Whenever I skip this step for some reason, usually because a client is short on time, the results are never as exciting. We still find great looking clothes, but don't go to that expressive next level.

Gather materials

Favorite fashion magazines and catalogs from department stores and specialty companies are the best source for images. If you don't have subscriptions, here's a tip: Most hair salons get rid of their beauty magazines at the end of every month. Tear out anything that catches your eye and save it in a file.

Be inspired

The beginnings of the spring and fall seasons are good times to focus on your relationship to current fashion. Impulses of all types are reason enough to get started, like a craving for a certain color, or seeking a connection to your body image. Sometimes words leap off the page at you. Add text or other types of images to your file, including fortunes from a cookie, your horoscope, a touching letter or greeting card, a scrap of poetry, a photocopy of a book cover, anything that resonates with you.

Edit

Lay out the pages you have ripped out onto the floor and stand over them. Edit out the less perfect or unnecessary. Stand back and take a second look. Wield your scissors and get rid of any part of the model or outfit you don't relate to. If you don't like her hair color or expression, then off with her head. Cut the image out to better define the shape.

Assemble

The simplest way to assemble a collage is to use a piece of 18 x24 inch poster board and a glue stick. If you would like to connect with color even further, try a little "art making." Get a big piece of watercolor paper and layer it with washes of watercolor or acrylic paint. You can focus on one family of color (reds, blues, greens, purples, neutrals, metallic gold and/or silver) or you can paint your personal rainbow. Another way to add color and texture is to buy a pack of multihued tissue paper. Dilute white glue with water and using an old paint brush, attach it to poster board. Use the sheets of tissue as backgrounds, or try layering the tissue over some of the images, overlapping them for a stained glass effect.

Use the language of self-expression

Use your journal to dialogue with yourself by looking at your collage and asking yourself the following questions:

Looking at my collage I see…?

My collage makes me feel…?

You may come up with some adjectives that help you articulate the words you want to use to describe yourself this season.

Enjoy using imagery to stimulate language. Here's an example:

Bursting forth, all blooms and blossoms, unfurling petals with their soft round edges, seeking and finding the light...Oceans of dark blue cool against the heat of summer, dusky blue-gray restful in the shade, pink and red warm, happy and playful. Reach out and touch her before she dances or floats away, but wait...she stops and stares directly at you with a gaze both humorous and knowing.

Keep your collages and watch your progression. Ask yourself: How has my spirit evolved since my last collage? What am I craving NOW?

My Personal Favorites for Images:

- **Magazines**

  Lucky, *Harper's Bazaar* and *Elle* have useful editorials, and I also use a smattering from the other magazines I read including *O*, *More*, *In Style* and *People*. Occasionally *W* and *Vogue* will have a great issue, but for the most part the layouts are too fantastic or outlandish to be of much practical use. But the ads are always good. *Glamour* and *Jane* are good for the under-forty crowd.

- **Catalogs**

  I am on the mailing list to receive catalogs for all of the major department stores in my area, including *Macy's*, *Nordstrom*, *Bloomingdales*, *Saks Fifth Avenue* and *Neiman-Marcus* and from smaller chain stores; including *Anthropologie*, *J.Jill*, *J.Crew*, *Lucy* and *Chico's*. *Victoria's Secret* has sexy lingerie, but beware, if you get on their mailing list you will be inundated with mail. Other useful mail order catalogs include: *Territory Ahead*, *Peruvian Connection*, *Boden*, *Land's End*, *Eddie Bauer*, *Coldwater Creek*, *REI*, *Soft Surroundings*, *Orvis*, *LL Bean*, *Athleta* and *Title Nine Sports*. Watch my Web site for updates.

Seek out playful colors that give you a sense of happy anticipation about the day ahead.

Part Five   ACT

making it happen

The mustard fields have suddenly sprung to life. Even in the watery winter light, smears of color brighten the landscape. Only yesterday we were surrounded by dormant winter grasses. Storm clouds threaten as our small band of artists hurriedly set up their easels.

The mustard fields radiate such an impossible yellow that I can't capture it in my painting. The experience of standing and looking at this field glowing with light is satisfaction enough. On this magical day, I'm rewarded for painting through the dull days of winter, for showing up, for staying. At this moment, I'm glad for all the days I hung in there and practiced when I felt like going home, putting in my time so that when the trees blossom and the earth springs to life I'll be ready. Later, I make several other attempts to paint the mustard, but none satisfy me. Still, the sensation of yellow fills my heart and I am bursting to express it, so I do something I never do. I write a poem.

MUSTARD SEA

For those who wait

Through the dark, drab afternoons

The light as flat as a blown out tire

As the earth lies dormant

There comes an awakening and

One day it is there

A yellow postage stamp

Seen from a distant window

If you go there

The clouds will part and in

The watery blue light

The mustard field glows

Nuclear

So impossibly yellow

So yellow there needs to be a new word

To describe this awakening

Prepare, and you will be rewarded like we were on the day the mustard burst into bloom. Put in your time; stick. You are ready – everything you have done so far has prepared you to get to this point. You are ready for the great adventure of shopping. Soon you will see yourself where you want to be, glowing with success.

shopping: the great adventure

BORN TO SHOP...OR NOT?

For me, recreational shopping is fun. It is a pleasure to stroll through little shops with a friend, see what's new and try on a few things if I feel like it, maybe happen upon an unexpected treasure. It's also a delight to wander the streets of a new city while on vacation, stepping inside an intriguing store to see what's there. Yet when it comes to the focused work of building or completing a wardrobe, personally I would rather be home reading a good book. I wish the perfect clothes would just materialize in my closet. I admit it. Despite my chosen profession, shopping is not my favorite thing to do, especially if I need to search for something missing from my wardrobe that also happens to be a fit challenge. At the same time, I am clear that the result of looking great in my clothes is a top priority.

Over the years I have occasionally longed to give up shopping for people, to only do color palettes and wardrobe consultations, to focus more on my painting. I tell myself it would easier and less of a struggle. Even though I have an exuberant personality, I tire easily, and shopping is physically demanding work.

I've continued to shop for clients for over twenty years because the results matter. My business, *Clothe Your Spirit,* would just be a cool philosophy if I didn't take my clients through the crucial steps of finding the right clothes. Shopping is about problem solving in real time, making it happen despite the obstacles. Work, yes indeed, but it is also exhilarating and rewarding. Assisting my clients with shopping, or teaching them to shop for themselves, means they will have the full experience of *Growing More Beautiful*.

The other reason I keep shopping professionally is that it keeps me in the fashion game. When I show up for a shopping appointment, I need to look good. Not perfect, not necessarily ready to walk the runway or appear on television, but pulled together in an updated outfit that is flattering and comfortable. It is a challenge for me to keep it up, to stay inventive and keep my look fresh. By shopping, I learn about myself, and what I need to do to help others. I'm constantly checking out new resources and places to shop, and ways to solve problems. My personal struggles are part of what makes it real.

This chapter invites you to learn what it takes to make shopping infinitely more successful. We are going for results, because when the results are good, nothing else is quite as exciting.

A good day shopping begins with an

understanding of what makes a day successful, what you can do to enhance your experience, and the pitfalls you want to avoid. Consider all of the preparation that has brought you to this point. So far we've looked at the expressive aspects of color, the language of personal style, and how to forge a better body image. We've dispelled myths about aging and encouraged you to make original color and style choices. On the practical end, we've worked through your closet, considered your lifestyle, and assessed your financial considerations. You are becoming more aware of how to make the most of your assets and overcome your fit challenges. To clarify what you want your clothes to look like, you've

created a collage of current images. List in hand, you are ready to go.

When I shop for my clients, I have all the information I need to get started before they arrive, including a set of their color swatches, notes on their lifestyle, a detailed description of their body type, adjectives that describe their essence, a portfolio of images and a budget. We have both done our homework and are eager to see the results.

In addition to advance preparation, a successful shopping day has a lot to do with attitude. When shopping by yourself or with others, keep in mind the following key ingredients for success:

⊙ Begin with realistic expectations, including how much time and money you have available.

⊙ Clarify your intention. The clearer the intention, the higher the level of success.

⊙ Know yourself: your strengths, the limits of your endurance and your patience.

⊙ Keep an open mind. If you see something great that is not on your list, consider it anyway.

No matter how prepared you are, the biggest pitfalls are unrealistic expectations, lack of focus, a narrow outlook and settling on something just to be done with it. I've emphasized that focusing on what you need is important, but don't make your parameters so limited that finding something is overly difficult. Let something surprising catch your eye, follow your excitement wherever it leads. You've taken the time to familiarize yourself with current fashion, so don't get stuck looking for something that has worked for you in the past but is no longer available.

Let something surprising catch your eye, follow your excitement wherever it leads.

READY, SET...WHERE TO GO?

Discovering the best places to shop for your budget, lifestyle, body type and fashion spirit is an ongoing quest. Nothing is more frustrating than needing clothes and coming home empty handed. You need to seek out the places where you will have the most success.

There are three main types of choices: large department stores, smaller chain stores and boutiques. Within those broad categories is a huge range of styles and prices. There are advantages and disadvantages to all stores, so let's discuss them.

The first places to eliminate are stores that carry merchandise obviously not right for you. There are local stores where I know the owner personally, appreciate the merchandise and would love to support them, but their clothes don't fit my needs or my body.

Nothing is harder on your confidence or wears you out faster than trying on clothes where you feel like something is wrong with you or your body. Even though I am not large, my curvy body is better suited to clothes that are more classically cut. I've been trying to wear low-rise jeans for years and they are not flattering, and skinny tops look skimpy instead of sexy. I buy the bulk of my wardrobe in department stores, because I have learned which manufacturers have great style and also fit my body.

At this time in my life, department stores also fit my time vs. money equation. I don't have as much time as I would like to seek out smaller stores. The other big plus the department stores offer is their return policy. I believe in making choices in the fitting room, but it is still nice to be able to bring garments home and make final decisions.

The problem with department stores is that the environment is so unfriendly. The lights, the music, the air quality, the seemingly endless racks of clothes, and the long, long distance to the door when you are dying for fresh air can make for an exhausting experience.

The smaller chain stores like *J. Jill, The Gap, Banana Republic, J Crew, Chico's, Ann Taylor* and *Anthropologie* have the advantages of both manageable size and a lenient return policy, which makes them a good option if you like their merchandise. They are often handily clustered together in malls. The European discount chains *H & M* and *Zara* are now available in select cities here in the U.S., so keep an eye out for them when you travel.

Popular tourist destinations, including the Bay Area and surrounding Wine Country, are full of interesting streets and plazas filled with specialty shops. Women who travel on business tell me that after a day of meetings, they like get to know a new area and supplement their wardrobe at the same time.

So, what to do and where to go? Find a happy mix. Even though I buy many of my foundation pieces at department stores, I love putting the icing on my cake with treasures from boutiques. I have favorites I regularly visit as a treat to myself, and I make a point to investigate somewhere new when I vacation.

Shopping from catalogs is another option. Be prepared to compromise on color and fit, and plan to spend time at the post office returning things. People who live outside major cities tell me it is their best alternative; but I suspect their time would be better spent planning a shopping trip a couple of times a year for their wardrobe basics and using catalogs to fill in. On the plus side, mail order from outdoor outfitters like *Patagonia, Land's End, LL Bean, Title Nine Sports, Lucy* and *REI* are great time savers for specialty items such as active wear and cold weather gear. Or, you might luck into a style that fits well that you can order in multiple colors.

Internet shopping sites have taken the industry by storm, especially for bargain hunters and those in need of specialty sizes. Zappos.com is my personal favorite for shoes because everything is fully refundable and they pay the shipping both ways. Bluefly.com is just one of the many sites my clients love for the great deals. Zafu.com will ask you questions about your preferences and body type and then suggest an appropriate jean or swimsuit style. Amazing! I even know a designer jean maniac who finds all her favorite styles on E-Bay.

One last reminder: Don't torture yourself by shopping somewhere that is out of your price range. Conversely, don't let guilt about cost lead you somewhere that doesn't carry the level of merchandise that will satisfy you. Watch for sales, or try a high-end consignment store.

ASK FOR HELP

I depend on honest, savvy, skilled sales people, both personally and professionally. I need their expertise about their stock to know how a garment is fitting.

I want to hear the truth about what looks good and what does not. Learn to seek out great sales people, and then trust them to help you solve your wardrobe challenges.

How do you know if a sales professional is being honest with you or just trying to make the sale? Your comfort level should tell you everything you need to know. Right away you should feel seen. Especially precious is someone who really sees what is beautiful about you and can help you find something flattering and expressive.

Not every person you work with will have this gift, but they can be of help in other ways. People who enjoy fashion love to put outfits together. They run through the store and bring you back options that turn your garments into ensembles. Some are great with color, others knowledgeable when it comes to fit. I love it when they surprise me with something I never would have considered.

Many department stores have in-house personal shoppers and I frequently use one, both for myself and for my clients. The biggest advantage of the in-house shopping services is that they are designed to help you create and complete your wardrobe. The personal shoppers move freely throughout the store, and choose items from many different departments. There is no charge for this service, and a personal shopper can help you no matter what your budget. Arrive for your appointment prepared with a clear idea of your priorities, and how much you can spend.

Most small-store owners strive to be aware of the needs of their clientele, and make conscious choices on their behalf. One owner told me, "I keep my

Wardrobing is having the specific layered, coordinated outfits to fulfill every obligation in your life. Having a lot of items that mix and match is not wardrobing.

clients in mind when I go to market, and make sure I choose a range of garments that will fit everyone." If you are a loyal customer, you will be remembered. Ask to be called when something special for you arrives.

Take care to avoid being swept up in someone else's enthusiasm. Learn to recognize the difference between honesty and flattery. If you ever feel pressured, tense or uncomfortable for any reason, take a break or make a hasty exit. If you love something but feel unsure, put it on hold and come back later, or return with a friend. Don't be shy about asking for what you need. Some small stores will allow you to take home merchandise on twenty-four hour approval, so you can see how it looks with what you have at home.

"Who would have thought a nineteen year old young man could be so helpful? He really knew his stuff. And the gal with the crazy multicolored hair at Anthropologie...she was fantastic! You never know by looking at someone if they are going to be helpful or not." Stacie

WARDROBING

"I love to shop, it is my favorite hobby. I thrill to the "hunt," looking for those special pieces, or finding something fabulous at a rock bottom price. I love to mix vintage with contemporary. The only problem is, I end up with too many pieces that don't go together and I have trouble coming up with complete outfits." Patricia

Remember, no matter where you choose to shop, it is important to try to create outfits instead of buying solo pieces. The most important thing my shopping clients learn from me is the concept of *wardrobing*. When I look inside someone's closet, the biggest problem I see is the variety of mismatched items that don't work together. Wardrobing is having the specific layered, coordinated outfits to fulfill every obligation in your life. Having a lot of items that mix and match is not wardrobing. Shopping for new clothes is your opportunity to remedy that. When you are in the fitting room, you need to constantly ask yourself the following questions:

- How does this fit in with what I have?
- Does this fill a gap in my wardrobe?
- Do I love it enough to find the necessary pieces, including shoes and accessories?
- Can I update it next year?

This brings us back to another of the big-store advantages, the ready availability of so many coordinating pieces. If you find a jacket or pants you like, see what goes with it. Carry it around with you to other departments. Color in fashion runs in cycles, with many designers using the same hues. Or wander out into the mall or shopping village and see what you can find.

A simple wardrobing tip is "think in threes." You have a top, a bottom, but the "third" piece is what makes the outfit. When you add a jacket, a vest, a cardigan, a shirt or a shawl, not only will your outfit provide you with the layering comfort you need, your look will be finished and complete.

Everyone always asks what a basic wardrobe consists of, and I think the answer is too individual to generalize. It depends upon how many complete outfits

you need for all the different aspects of your life. Generally, you do need more tops than bottoms, and you need multiples of anything that needs to be cleaned frequently. Decide if you are happier with the simplicity of fewer pieces worn more frequently,

or if you love to play with a plethora of alternatives.

Develop a plan for getting started. Let's say it is a new season and you are ready to start fresh. Once you have assessed your wardrobe you will know what you need to do, but it helps to take a flexible approach so you don't get discouraged and head home empty handed.

When you start to feel that your foundation is taking shape, consider what might jazz up your ensembles. We'll be talking about the importance of accessories

in the next section, but don't miss an opportunity to add pizzazz and flair with interesting color and texture combinations.

SHOPPING ALCHEMY

After all the planning that goes into taking myself or a client shopping, at some point the specific information becomes a dull roar in the background, subtext to the actual drama of the day. The alchemical aspect of shopping takes over. A shopping trip becomes a mix of what is in the store that moment, the shopper's mood, even the weather. Usually what happens is anything but straightforward, and the path will take interesting, unexpected turns.

A woman needs to bring her inner artist to the fitting room and let the creative process take hold. I do meticulous preparation for my appointments, but when I am roaming the store I am wide open to the possibilities, looking for pieces that are pretty, unusual, different, exciting, striking in some way. I look at mannequins for inspiration and adapt what appeals to me. When I bring all these special pieces into the fitting room, I start experimenting. I see how far I can stretch the use of color, what unusual combinations of shapes and textures I can put together. I do this for people with the simplest of lifestyles, looking at how the ordinary can become the extraordinary.

The art is in the mix. You have a window into seeing the diversity within your own being. Extend that into how you choose your clothing. Combine classic slacks with a crazy vest from the junior department.

SHOPPING MEDITATION

If at some point during your trip you are starting to feel overwhelmed, take a break. Close the door to your fitting room, sit down, relax your eyes, take a few deep breaths and go inward. Tune out the craziness of your immediate environment and let the artist in you daydream for a moment. Go to a place where your reactions are spontaneous and non-judgmental, where your imagination has free rein. Think back to your collage, and remember the kinds of looks that attracted you. Visualize a beautiful scene in nature that is part of the season you are currently in. Deep blue skies, autumn leaves, wet bark, the ocean, juicy spring green grass, gorgeous flowers, a flaming sunset. Imagine an exquisite piece of artwork that touched you, or the furnishings of a handsome interior. Let a longing for something beautiful blossom inside you. This is your chance to make choices that help you feel connected to the beauty of the world around you. Now go out there and find it.

In the fitting room all I want to do is play dress up, not think about trekking through stores with my clients or getting muddy with my dog.

Add a designer original to your favorite find from the clearance rack. Mix practical with fanciful, slouchy menswear with frills, workout wear with velvet and cashmere. Remember balance and proportion, and to create a focal point. My preference is for your face to always be the center of interest, but you can do whatever you like. If it is an authentic reflection of your spirit, it will work. Fashion is just an opportunity to express your individuality. Whose right is it to say if something does or doesn't work for you? You are standing up for your choices and developing your ability to see. Who better to decide?

People have a fantasy that artists love to sling paint around, but our approach is usually disciplined and yours should be too. But we all live for those wild moments of pure experience.

DECIDING WHAT TO BUY

A garment that is perfect for you helps you fall in love with yourself, your face, your body, your unique essence. When that happens, an unequivocal YES bubble bursts inside you. You know in an instant if something is right for you. The rest of the time that you are "deciding" is actually spent talking yourself into a garment that you've convinced yourself you need or appeals to you in some way but isn't exactly right. It can be a challenge getting to the point of recognizing and honoring the clear YES, but you can acknowledge the obvious - that it's taking an awfully long time to decide. Accept the fact the garment just isn't right and you are trying to talk yourself into it. Something totally new and unexpected might give you a moment's pause, but it should be followed with a flood of delight. If you aren't sure until you see what goes with it, then try to find something that will resolve that question for you.

The person advising you, whether friend or professional, is going to have an influence. If you are going to listen to his or her opinion, make sure it's someone you trust. Do you feel special and attractive when you are with that person? Even if a salesperson appears knowledgeable and experienced, it doesn't mean his or her advice is right for you. If you feel uncertain or uncomfortable, don't allow yourself to be talked into something.

Growing More Beautiful is dependent upon cultivating and honoring your intuitive responses. You can feel in your gut if something is right for you or not. Ask yourself:

- Does it fit perfectly?
- Is it comfortable, non-binding and made from soft fabric?
- Is this what I really want?
- Is this how I want to look? Is it ME?
- Do I want to rip the tag off and wear it NOW?
- Will the type of shoes I like to wear work with this look?
- Am I prepared to spend the money on the necessary alterations?
- Is this something I will really wear, or a fantasy item that will hang forlornly in my closet?

Ouch, I hate that last one. I love glamorous, fancy, party clothes. I look my best in velvet, fur, beaded and sparkling sweaters. I love novelty skirts alive with wonderful patterns and designs that look like works of art. Strapless sundresses á la Marilyn

Monroe seem perfect for summer. In the fitting room all I want to do is play dress up, not think about trekking through stores with my clients or getting muddy with my dog.

Alas, reality intrudes. Busy lives demand wearable clothes, but don't give in to the burning desire to find something you need and just be done with it. If you compromise at all on fit, the garment will be the first to be in the discard heap a year from now. It is worth being patient until you find just what you are looking for. Mistakes are costly to both your pocketbook and self-esteem.

The time has arrived to make your final decisions. Choose only the best of the best. If your shopping day is going quite well, trim the excess and decide what you can't live without. Look for duplicates and discard them first. Try to keep your coordinate groups, (all the pieces that go together) intact. If you are still over budget, take a deep breath and imagine what you would be genuinely sorry to leave behind, and eliminate the rest. On the other hand, if you find yourself wishing you had stayed home, make a beeline for the door and try again another day. Don't buy something just because you have spent a lot of time or your ego is bruised and you want to make it feel better. The time you've spent looking was certainly not wasted. It's helped you focus and eliminate what you don't want so that the path to what you do want is clearer.

It is a challenge to decide right there and then what to buy and what to leave behind, especially if you are tired. If the store has a liberal return policy, you may ask yourself, why not just get it all?

The answer is peace of mind. If you have the courage to make a decision in the moment, you will be rewarded with the pleasure of completing your task and being able to move on and think about something else. If you trundle home a bunch of clothes you are uncertain about, you will have to deal with them a few more times before you finally return them. This lack of clarity creates weighty, obsessive thoughts, dragging you downward into a negative spiral.

Don't worry about doing it perfectly, but do your best to stay focused and respond to your inner voice. If you do get something home and in the light of a new day it feels less than exciting, take it back. Don't compromise. "Catch and release" is a fly-fishing term, and that is exactly what you are going to do. Fishermen use barbless hooks to cause no harm to the fish, so don't be hard on yourself. Adios, no big deal, better luck next time.

PERSEVERANCE FURTHERS

No matter what the outcome of a shopping day, don't get overly discouraged, and by all means, don't give up. "Seat time" is what pilots call the countless hours they must spend training in an airplane in order to get their "ticket." Seat time applies to any endeavor that involves showing up.

Practice and persistence pay off, but rarely in a straightforward way. Every time I complete a painting that doesn't work, I toss it on the pile and remind myself that I am putting in some "seat time." Another day spent practicing. Still, it is frustrating not to be able to capture my vision on paper. When I get over my disappointment with the outcome of the painting, I study it to see what I can do differently next time.

Learn to sort out feelings into information. Analyze what isn't working for you. Do you need more information, a new approach or a different selection of stores? Remember that the words "creative" and "process" are intrinsically linked. In this case "process" means it might take a while. The shopping practices I am describing might be totally new for you. Give yourself some time to get the hang of it, or get some help. Your perseverance will get you where you want to go.

Success builds confidence and finding terrific clothes is its own reward. The results of a great day shopping make it all worthwhile. I get totally jazzed helping my clients put together wonderfully expressive, practical outfits. I'm thrilled to find a gorgeous garment for myself, or that perfect item that suddenly makes multiple pieces work together. I may have to return shoes that don't feel good when I wear them around the house, but ultimately I find great ones that do.

If shopping were easy, there wouldn't be professionals like me helping others. Luckily, these skills can be learned. I cannot imagine a worse scenario than every client I have ever taken shopping coming back to me, season after season, for ongoing assistance. What a nightmare to imagine twenty years of clients, all wanting an appointment at the same time. Fortunately, most of my clients get the hang of shopping for themselves and move on. I have to admit, I miss many of them, but my little birdies must fledge the nest. Early in my career I made a decision that my services were always to be educational in nature, by empowering women and men to understand the process of clothing their spirits.

A few clients work with me indefinitely because they find our collaboration supportive, creative and inspiring, and frankly, they can afford it. They are the exception. My other clients eventually begin shopping on their own with a great deal more information than when we first began working together. They know what colors they look great in and what styles suit them. They have more insight into the needs of their lifestyle and have a good idea of where to shop. After a season or two of shopping together, they understand the concept of wardrobing, and how to build on what they have. Many come back every few years for a refresher, but it is gratifying to know they have been able to supplement their wardrobes on their own.

Learn to sort out feelings into information.

Jeans are in a class by themselves.

Remember seat time, but don't forget play time. Take inspiration from Jane and Elisabeth, who call their shopping trips their "naughty girl escapades." They hit the stores all day, providing each other with supportive advice and plenty of chocolate. Leslie and Marti schedule a shopping day together every season. I know some great mother/daughter teams, and some incredible husbands with superb taste and unbelievable patience. You can teach your friends how to be helpful, and find out how to be helpful to them in return. Respect each other's energy level, pace yourself, and don't forget to bring water. Be sure to keep your energy from flagging by taking a break for a nourishing lunch, a restorative cup of tea or a chocolate chip cookie.

My wish is for you to find an approach to shopping that works for you, so that your experiences grow more successful and rewarding over time, allowing you to reveal the beautiful creation that you are.

"I'm a full-time painter and art teacher, and I don't need much, but I do need clothes. Before you came along and helped me get ready for my trip to Europe and my daughter's wedding, I wasn't aware of my clothes. I knew I needed new ones, but since I didn't have a plan I would postpone dealing with it. Now I've found an approach that works for me. I set aside an afternoon and spend several hours focusing on shopping. I'm six feet tall, so my height is a challenge. I start with shoes. I like the outlet mall in Napa, because they have a couple of shoe stores that carry the type of shoes I enjoy wearing. Then I move on to
J. Crew, because I know their size 16 pants fit me and are long enough. The skirts and shorts at Ann Taylor also fit me well. I buy most of what I need for the season: shoes, sweaters, pants, tops, shorts, a skirt or a dress. I find if I buy them at the same time I am conscious of coordinating everything. This time I even bought a purse."* Joan

"I popped into Nordstrom Rack today and found a dress I absolutely adore. It's a chocolate brown color with an off-white circle pattern, kind of mod, hip-looking fabric. It is stretchy with little cap sleeves and a v-neck and gathers in the middle and it fits perfectly. As I was driving home I realized how much more confident I feel about choosing things. I wasn't wearing sleeveless or fitted things until we met, and I certainly wasn't enjoying or nurturing my style. It was so much fun to go into a store, know my correct size, look for a dress that might work and then trust my opinion when I found one I loved. I also found a jacket in a perfect blue color but it was a tiny bit too small so I reluctantly put that back on the rack, knowing if it doesn't fit it isn't worth buying even if the color is awesome." Julie

THE HOLY GRAIL OF DENIM

Jeans are in a class by themselves. In less than fifty years they have gone from a working man's staple to a status symbol. I was tempted to include jeans in the Body Image section of this book because our feelings about how we look in our jeans are similarly complex.

I love jeans. There are always multiple pairs of jeans in my closet, and yes, they all fit. I have comfy pairs for hanging around and sleeker pairs for going out. I have different rises and waist treatments to pair with different tops, different lengths for boots or flats, different weights and washes for different seasons. I like that you can machine wash and dry them, that they can look both sexy and informal, and that they toughen up and make more casual whatever you put with them. I also like that they are not such a big investment so I can update the shape whenever I want a fresh new style or I have gained a few pounds. I like the curve hugging feel when they fit just right. For jeans to fit snugly enough to look attractive, something usually gets squeezed, so finding one flattering pair can mean trying on dozens.

I have never found a pair of premium denim jeans that were so fabulous they made me want to shell out hundreds of dollars for them. It doesn't mean it will never happen, but I've stopped searching for the Holy Grail of Denim, the pair of jeans that looks so amazing that unbeknownst to me all my other pairs were pitiful "befores."

I think every woman who likes jeans should own a few flattering pairs, and should update her jeans wardrobe frequently. With the wide variety of shapes and sizes, there is a pair to fit everyone. I'm just not convinced that the miracle pair is out there waiting, just beyond your reach, and that you should go in search of them.

I've found moderately priced jeans that look fine. Even though I have seen jean "makeovers" on Oprah and in countless style magazines, it has been darn infrequent that I actually see a woman whose jeans look amazing. Check it out for yourself. The next time you are people watching, pay particular attention to the parade of denimed behinds. You'll see surprisingly few women who look sensational. The reason for this is that no matter how you dress them up, jeans are stiff heavy cotton with or without a touch of spandex. Of all the fabrics available, heavy cotton is not especially forgiving or flattering. Lycra is great for comfort, but it doesn't always hold its shape, causing the fabric to stretch and bag. Denim often bunches rather than smoothes. So don't be so hard on yourself (or your poor beleaguered bottom) if you haven't found the perfect pair.

On the other hand, my thirty-three year old sister-in-law doesn't agree. On a recent shopping trip together, she swore if I would try on a hundred pairs I would find The One. Josie lives to find the perfect pair of jeans. She pairs them with casual tee-tops and flat shoes. The idea of spending a lot of money on a blouse or sweater seems silly to her. Why waste it on a top when you can buy a great pair of jeans instead? How the jeans fit over her curves is the most important statement she can make. Spending the biggest chunk of her clothing budget makes sense for her, as it does for her friends. I could say it is the age gap between us, except I know there are many women over fifty who feel the same way. It is all about priorities and we are each doing what feels right to us.

P.S. While you are watching the denim parade pass by, notice how many women are wearing black tops.

"I'm happy with my Banana Republic contour fit jeans, but everyone was talking about this fabulous jeans shop in Santa Barbara, so I thought I would check it out. I couldn't find anything, but the good thing was I knew that the store had nothing right for my body, not that somehow my body wasn't right. The last pair I tried on was funny. The girl was getting frustrated not finding jeans for me and she said, "Here is a great pair for you but you have to really work yourself into them." So I did and when I came out, poured into them, she said "Those are perfect for you!" I laughed and said, "Honey, I am too smart to work this hard to get into jeans." You and I would have laughed hysterically." Leslie

SWIMWEAR–HOW TO STRUT YOUR STUFF

My husband Jerry offered me a deal. He would help me pick out a swimsuit and he would pay for it if I let him choose the winner. I was more than a little skeptical about this plan, especially when he went right for the two-piece suits. I tried to tell him I never wore a bikini even when I was a teen. I didn't have a two-piece swimsuit kind of a body, I protested. He ignored me. I can still remember the salesperson helping us that day, looking over her glasses at us and saying what we had chosen were "junior swimsuits." How embarrassing.

But her comment emboldened me. So what? Jerry picked out a yellow, orange and red string bikini with a matching mini skirt printed with a tropical sunset. When I wore that suit I was surprised how comfortable I felt in it. I've let Jerry pick out all my

suits since, from zebra striped tankinis, to one-piece suits with audacious cut outs. The young sales girls think we are fun. We have attitude.

I try to serve the same function for my clients. I'm their Jerry. We all need someone to advocate for us and our near naked bodies. The following are my favorite strategies for selecting a swimsuit.

Jennifer and Jerry's Top Ten Tips for Choosing a SwimSuit

1. Shop where they specialize in swimwear and have lots of selection. Don't slink in and out, hoping no one will see you. Enlist the aid of someone helpful and enthusiastic. Keep your focus and sense of humor. Tell them you want something fabulous. Or take someone with you, someone positive and a little outrageous, a slyly evil twin that will make you show off your body-luscious.

2. Get the suit tight enough to support you. Go down a size and see if it still fits. It is going to loosen up when it gets wet. *"Keep going down a size until you can't get it on."* Jerry

3. Try on lots and lots of different styles. If your top and bottom are different sizes, buy pieces that are sized separately.

4. Pick a luscious color that makes you happy. Don't feel you have to buy black because it makes you look thinner. Imagine yourself on your breezy, sun splashed getaway. Look around you, do you see anything black? A great color will enhance your skin tone and give you confidence.

5. Get some great accessories to go with your new suit; a fun cover-up, flip flops, beach bag and hat. Get a spray tan and a pedicure, maybe even an anklet and temporary tattoo. Now you're fabulous!

6. If you don't want to expose your tummy, try a one-piece with strategically paced cut outs. They give your belly some coverage, but still look risky and sexy and outrageous. If your thighs bother you, cover them with a skirt that is flirty and fun while you draw the attention elsewhere. *"If you don't want to expose your tummy or your thighs, see tip #10."* Jerry

7. If sporty is more your look, get stylized sporty. Don't go for a utilitarian Speedo except for swimming laps. Exaggerate the sporty look with a belt or dramatic color blocking.

8. When you are shopping, every time you groan, you must also laugh. Laughing five times for every time you feel like groaning is even better.

9. Admire the women who aren't thin but are still strutting their stuff. Listen for what foreign language they are speaking because it probably won't be English.

10. *"It isn't hard to figure out the parts that need showing off and then show 'em off. There will always be a suit that will do that. Focus on the under-appreciated parts of your body. Get a suit that features them, as opposed to one that hides and minimizes and pretends they don't exist. You will have the pleasure of finding out that what you considered a liability is actually an asset. One of the jobs of a bathing suit is to show your self-confidence. Just remember your curves are in the 'normal' range, there is nothing extreme about them. Hiding shows in your face and body language, so strut your stuff."* Jerry

Note: Jerry says he is available for consultations, just as long as no purses or scarves are involved. Or send a photo to www.BathingSuitJerry.com.

"Dear Bathing Suit Jerry,
Thanks for the bathing suit consultation. I took your advice and ordered a lemon yellow string bikini from Victoria's Secret. It came in the mail yesterday and I tried it on. I ordered two sizes so I could have a smaller option as you noted in your bathing suit tips. You were right........it looked pretty good. Maybe better than that. I put it on and casually walked past my husband as he was on the computer and asked if he thought it was ok. I wish I had a picture of the look on his face. Anyway, I just wanted to tell you that your advice was right on and a big confidence booster for me. As promised, I will send you a picture, and I will keep you updated on future suits. Love, Les"

Part Six PERSONALIZE

Playtime

It is only the beginning of February, and already the bare branches of the cherry trees are sporting little buds. It looks as though the blossoms will grace us early this year. I giddily welcome the arrival of their flirty pinkness, adorning the trees like a ballerina's ruffled tutu.

I hurry home to my art studio, where a table is laden with greeting-card-making supplies. Valentine's Day is less than two weeks away, and I have a long list of loved ones. Making valentines is something I look forward to every year, a time of pure childlike pleasure and play for me.

The shape of the heart is so simple, and a mere sprinkle of glitter makes it into something special. The shape of luscious lips puckered into a kiss is always a welcome addition. There is no such thing as a poorly composed valentine, no unappreciated message of sensuality and love.

Get out the glitter and put a little love on your heart!

the beauty of accessories

Ahhh, accessories. How I warm to this subject! My inner artist is jumping up and down with excitement. Accessories are deliciously inspiring additions to your wardrobe. After the hard work of shopping, we now get to turn your closet into a playground. Yippee!

PULLING IT TOGETHER

After a shopping trip you will want to regroup, to look at your purchases with a fresh eye. Expect some revision. It is impossible to be totally accurate on a buying trip.

I often meet with clients for a follow-up appointment where we look over what we have purchased in natural light and see what is needed to complete each ensemble. Each item is tried on with proper undergarments, and we check to see if alterations are necessary. Then we start to play; adding, subtracting, trying on a necklace here, a unique belt there. With every change we stand back to get the complete view in order to discern what works the best.

Looking at yourself fully clothed and accessorized is your opportunity to make sure the eye travels fluidly from your head to your feet and back to your face again. A successful painting has a focal point, and the eye moves around the canvas, never going off the edge of the canvas or getting stuck in one spot. In this case your face is the focal point, and we also want the viewer to take pleasure in the length of you, taking in all the beauty before it happily returns to your face.

JEWELRY

My favorite accessories are great jewelry and a fabulous lipstick. These two things never fail to lift my spirits when I look in the mirror. I love jewelry for the way it makes the wearer more beautiful and expressive. Even if I am mucking about I can still wear all the sparkles I want. Great personal jewelry makes a statement. Jewelry helps you to show up. It introduces you to everyone you come into contact with. Women comment on each others earrings as a way of saying hello. As jewelry designer Simma Chester says, *"The perfect piece of jewelry that is right for you looks good with a ball gown or with jeans."*

Jewelry can be interesting, dramatic or distinctive in its own right, but my preference is for pieces that enhance the individuality and attractiveness of the wearer. Color, shape and design echo and enhance your coloring and features, repeating and reinforcing your assets. Colored stones bring out eyes, lips and cheeks. Creamy pearls glow against the skin. Earrings enhance the structure of your face, flattering your jawline and showing off the length of your neck. Both bracelets and earrings add movement and sparkle.

Jewelry can take a simple garment and give it presence, turning the ordinary into the extraordinary. If you have always chosen jewelry that is understated and classic and would like to branch out and try something more expressive, you can begin by connecting with your Spirit Terms. Pearls and semiprecious stones are *luminous,*
elegant, natural, warm, cool and refined. Stones that are faceted have more *sparkle,* but in their natural state they can be *rich* and *earthy.* The design of a piece of jewelry can be *sensuous, delicate, fluid and gypsy-like.* If you're drawn to shape more than color, metals can be *clean*, *bold*, *edgy* or *dramatic*. Glass beads, buttons, charms and bright plastic shapes can be *playful, fresh and winsome*. An artful piece of jewelry often has a mix of elements not unlike the yin/yang qualities of the spirit.

Notice what styles of jewelry appeal to you. Ask someone wearing a piece you admire for the name of the artist who created it. Fashion magazines often lead you to the Web sites of the jewelers they feature. Smaller clothing boutiques have jewelry and accessories that suit their clothing, and occasionally they will host jewelry trunk shows for visiting artists. There are galleries that specialize in art to wear, including jewelry and other artful accessories, like hats and scarves. One of my clients attends the annual professional artisan craft fair at San Francisco's Ft. Mason. She says, "Every year I spend the day there with a couple of my friends. We encourage each other to try something new and lend support. I always end up with a treasure I love."

The price for one of a kind, handmade pieces varies. If you fall in love with something but the price makes you gasp, keep in mind that you will be wearing it for years to come, long after the outfit you are coordinating it with is gone. Remind yourself what you spent on a single pair of shoes. If purchasing a piece of wearable art isn't appropriate

The perfect piece of
jewelry that is right for
you looks good with a
ball gown or with jeans.

One of the important aspects of jewelry is scale. Scale is to jewelry what proportion is to clothing.

for you, you can find great "faux-art" pieces at department stores and smaller chain stores like Chico's to spice up your outfits.

A great way to start experimenting is with a long necklace. Often called "Opera" length and approximately 44 to 50 inches long, this length is especially versatile. Worn long it is easy and relaxed, and when doubled it makes a more classic statement. In the chapter on fit I talked about the down vest I chose for petite Ellie. The vest had a sheen to it, and to complete her outfit of vest, plaid slacks and a sweater I added a long "rope" of freshwater pearls mixed with gold and silver beads. The luminous color of the pearls tied all the elements together, and the vertical line they created was visually lengthening. Worn long, the necklace gave Ellie the "dressy casual" feeling she was after. Ellie could also double the same necklace and pair it with a suit jacket and blouse for a more professional look.

Even if a piece of jewelry isn't the centerpiece of the outfit, you can use it to direct the eye to where you want it to go I favor necklines that are either scooped or v-shaped, and if the top is dark and has long sleeves, my chest area looks too blank. As much as I love my cleavage, I don't want my bare upper chest to be the focal point of my outfit. Just as a painter would use a brushstroke of color to blend an area that has too much contrast, a necklace of either silver or blue-gray pearls will break up the blank space and allow the eye to follow the line of the necklace back to my face where the color and sheen connects with my eyes and hair. If

you are wearing a solid color and the contrast with your skin is too stark, use jewelry to lighten up the look and bring in some needed animation.

One of the important aspects of jewelry is scale. Scale is to jewelry what proportion is to clothing. Obviously the same necklace that looks appropriate on a woman six feet tall would overwhelm someone petite. That doesn't mean a small woman should wear jewelry that is dainty and diminutive. Michelle wears a size 2 petite, but she has high cheekbones and striking features. She favors pieces that are chunky and dramatic. Connie is a larger woman (size 16) and enjoys intricately beaded pieces that are delicate and sensual. What makes each piece work for these two women is that the size, or scale, of each piece suits their bone structure and  stature. I wish there was an easy rule of thumb to help you decide what scale of jewelry is just right for you, but with practice (or some good advice) you will know it when you see it. With jewelry there is always an "ah-ha" or "ooh-ah" moment. If you own a piece of jewelry and like the materials but have never enjoyed wearing it, the scale might be the problem. See if a designer can suggest a way to remake it so you feel more excited about it.

Think of your jewelry as an ensemble cast, players that enhance and support each other. If your necklace makes a bold statement, keep your earrings simple. Choose a component of the necklace and repeat it in the earring. If your earrings are interesting, just add a bracelet or two. There is no need to match exactly; in fact, the art is always in the mix. Stand back and look in your full-length mirror, making sure you have chosen a focal point and harmonizing backdrop. The ideal is for the eye to move easily from one element to the next, always returning to your face.

I enjoy spending time creating a balance between all the ingredients in my outfits, and the way I wear my jewelry reflects my personal sensibility. Your style may be totally different. Pile it on if that's what suits you! I see other women loaded with layers of necklaces and bracelets and they look fabulous. And not everyone is drawn to jewelry. I once met the esteemed designer Eileen Fisher, and told her how I loved to use her clothing as a backdrop or canvas for jewelry. She demurred, telling me that she preferred the Zen simplicity of her designs worn simply and unadorned. You might prefer jewelry that is classic and understated, sleek and simple, chunky and dramatic. Honor whatever feels right as an expression of your spirit.

SHOES

There are two kinds of women: Those who love shoes and buy too many, and the rest of us who struggle to find something comfortable. Searching for shoes that are both stylish and wearable is an important part of my business. Shoes are the article of clothing most fundamental to your well-being. Uncomfortable shoes suck the joy right out of my day. The bottom line for comfort-loving women is that if the shoes aren't comfy, you won't wear the outfit.

If clothes are easier to find than shoes, set aside shopping sessions where shoes are the only focus. Ask for recommendations, go to favorite locations, and enlist good sales help. I think it is important to be able to take your new shoes home and walk around the house for an hour to be certain they fit comfortably, so consider the return policy when making your purchase.

Shoes are also a fabulous way to add personality to an outfit. A colorful or print shoe pops. Be discerning if your outfit has other interesting features. The following are a couple of examples that will help determine if a novelty shoe adds or detracts from the overall look.

When going through Barbara's closet, we both loved her animal print flats. We tried them on with her most playful outfit, a pair of brown cropped pants and matching cropped sweater paired with a contrasting lacy peach top. The shoes were the perfect shape and color, but when she looked in the mirror she said, *"It looks like I am trying too hard."* Because of the color and pattern on the top, multiple elements were vying for attention simultaneously, and the result was not the elegant but playful chic Barbara was looking for. When we substituted a simple shell in a coordinating warm toast color, the shoes were perfect, adding just the right accent.

Connie was accenting a white linen ensemble with luscious red coral jewelry for an upcoming cruise. Her red sandals didn't work, and neither did her coral red handbag. The dramatic color and style of the jewelry asked for a simple, uncluttered background and the red shoes were too much competition, moving the eyes away from Connie's pretty face. Better to stick with a neutral shoe that didn't draw attention. Or, switch to jewelry with just a touch of red, say in the earrings, and let the red shoes be the bright pop of color.

I'd feel dishonest if I didn't add this one last comment on shoes: When it comes to comfort, do as I say, not as I always do. I must admit to occasionally succumbing to the siren song of a beautiful shoe. If they are at all bearable, I'll navigate the parking lot as I walk from the car to the restaurant. These special shoes make me feel happy for some reason and not guilty that I only walk in them for minutes and not hours.

HANDBAGS, BELTS, SCARVES, HATS AND MORE!

Scarves, shawls, hats, fun socks and hosiery, whimsical hair clips, anything at all (including tiaras and crowns), are all ways to add interest to your outfit and express your personality. Knitting is currently all the rage and I can see why. Getting lost among the multicolored skeins of yarn at a knitting store is nirvana. Fabric and craft stores are another avenue to explore if you are handy with your hands. I am in awe of people who sew. Even if you are not an experienced seamstress you can still create

something simple. Have fun wandering the aisles, touching the bolts of fabric, daydreaming about all the beautiful things that could be made.

When completing your outfit be sure to attend to all the obvious details. If your skirt or pants have visible belt loops, then a coordinating belt is a must. Belts can also add shape and distinction to a garment, and can serve as an eye catching focal point. When you look in your full-length mirror, notice the role the metal belt buckle plays in your overall look. Either play it up with other metallic accents, or if it is too distracting, exchange it for a belt with a covered buckle. If you wear a stunning belt, don't create two centers of interest by wearing a necklace. The eye will bounce between one element and the other, and you want to keep it moving fluidly. The best bet is to keep the rest of your jewelry simple, adding only earrings or perhaps a bracelet.

Your handbag is an integral part of your overall look. Seeing a worn-out bag with a knot in the shoulder strap literally makes me cringe. Look in a full-length mirror to assess if the shape of the bag relates to your structure and form. The bag should curve where you curve, and sit comfortably next to your body. Pay attention to scale and avoid anything too large or too small. Keep trying until you feel satisfied that you have created a balanced proportion.

Deciding what type of bag to carry is of course a matter of personal preference. I like clean looking classic shapes, not too big, and I also carry a good looking tote to lug water, snacks and client files. I always keep an eye out for a gorgeous color that

will coordinate with my wardrobe, and I love finding something unexpected and playful to use during the summer months. As much as I love a beautiful bag, my personal preference is to put my serious money into jackets, shoes and jewelry. An expensive status "It" bag doesn't excite me.

Playing with accessories is less of a skill and more of an art, a way to exercise your creativity. Think of it as an adventure, with you always on a safari for something unique and special. A great purse can turn up in a luggage store or at a beachwear kiosk. Gardening centers are full of nifty gloves and waterproof boots. I could probably find something while waiting for my husband as he looked for car

parts. Hey, where do you think the inspiration for purses made from seat belts came from?

GOING THE DISTANCE

Go the distance with your wardrobe and finish up what you have started. If you wish to be beautifully dressed, you need to pay attention to the subtle details. Altering your clothes so that they fit properly is an absolute must. Ask a nicely-dressed neighbor for a referral, or see which seamstresses the boutiques in your area use. Save time by having your garments altered at the department store where you purchased them. Your local cleaners should do a respectable job on pant hems.

When I do a follow-up appointment in someone's closet I bring my camera along to photograph the finished outfits. My clients find it's invaluable to be able to refer back to the photos. Take some notes for yourself, or better yet, lay your outfits on the bed and take a photograph. Then hang your treasures in plain sight so you can mix and match and reinvent combinations whenever you feel like it. I try not to play when I am getting ready for work, but if I have a few extra minutes I can't resist experimenting, looking for different ways to adorn the canvas of my outfit. If I am undecided, I put my lipstick on just to get the full effect of the addition of that last punch of color. And then I smile at myself. Wow!

"I've been feeling a little pale and yucky lately and in need of a lift. I decided to get out my knitting needles but didn't have any yarn on hand that was really grabbing me, so I went to a yarn store – equipped with my color palette of course!!! It took me about five minutes to find the most beautiful yarn with all the blues and greens in my colors. Then I made the scarf in about two hours — using these huge salad tosser needles that I decided to try. I'm all about fast projects right now with the kids being little and no time to sit and knit. Anyway, I LOVE the scarf. When I wrapped it around my neck and looked in the mirror I saw that it looked awesome — even with my dark circles." Julie

Part Seven   POLISH

facetime

I like to paint subjects whose beauty makes my heart ache, and a face will do that to me every time. Painting a portrait is surprisingly similar to painting a landscape. Features have top, side and front planes just like hillsides and trees. Distances are measured, but in millimeters instead of miles. Light plays across the face the same way the sun arcs through the sky of a landscape, casting shadows on the nose and lower lip, creating dimension.

Doing a portrait that resembles the model is an interesting challenge. When I do a self-portrait, I'm not all that concerned in capturing my exact likeness. My hair becomes purple waves of amethyst and pearly lavender. My eyes are deep aquamarine pools, my lips plump ruby rosebuds. I'm intrigued by the quirky shape of my nose, with its bump in the middle and ball shape at the end. I discover the portrait doesn't look anything like me without the shadows under my eyes and the character lines around my nose and mouth.

Drawing my own likeness is my chance to create perfection, but instead I'm drawn to a version that is part fantasy, part reality and somehow captures the essence of my spirit.

Chapter Thirteen
make-up

〰️〰️〰️〰️〰️〰️〰️〰️〰️〰️〰️〰️〰️

ART FOR THE FACE

Early in my career I took my clients to department stores to help them select make-up, but my discerning eye for color was never satisfied, and it wasn't long before I started my own line. For a small company I carry way too many colors, and I would probably notice I wasn't making much of a profit if I ever bothered to check.

I don't care. Make-up is something too important to compromise on. The right color allows make-up to appear to melt into the skin, looking virtually invisible except for the enhancement it provides.

Selecting the perfect color isn't the only important factor. Over the years I've found that the ease of application determines whether make-up will be worn or left to languish in a drawer untouched. Application needs to be effortless, the scent pleasant, and the product and tools must feel good to the

touch. Your individual preferences determine what you will enjoy wearing.

Applying make-up is a sensuous pleasure. You should love how you look when you have finished your application, noticing the beauty of your features far more than the make-up itself.

Your face is like a canvas. Foundation, concealer, brow pencil and blush are your support, the background for the focal points of your lips and eyes. You can play up either your eyes or lips, adding stronger color for emphasis, or you can create a balance between the two.

After over twenty years as a make-up artist and creator of my own line, make-up is something I could talk about at great length. For the sake of brevity, here are some general guidelines. The following suggestions are my preferences. All make-up artists use different techniques and products they favor.

FREQUENTLY ASKED QUESTIONS

Q. What is the best type of foundation?

A. The one that you will wear. A foundation in a perfect match to your skin tone smoothes out imperfections and when blended with fingers, sponge or foundation brush makes a wonderful canvas. The newer mineral powders also even out the skin and have the added benefit of a chemical-free sunscreen. They are not irritating and reduce inflammation. Quickly applied with a brush, they are hugely popular because they are fast, easy and feel weightless. All my "playground moms" love them.

Q. What do you consider the most important products to use?

A. A good concealer is a must, especially for dark circles and sunspots. It really helps you look fresher and younger. Look for the best coverage you can find, in a color that blends easily with your skin tone. A yellow-tinged concealer is useful to counteract the blue in your under eye shadows. Using other products depends on you and your features. Brows are crucial for framing the eye and adding balance and dimension to the rest of your features. A pencil softly defines, and a powdered brow color with a stiff brush fills in gaps. I carry a brow tint that is like mascara for light colored or graying brows, and it comes in several colors. Or it is a great option if you color your hair. I can't leave the house without eyeliner, but for me mascara is optional. I save it for important work days and special occasions. I also think lip liner and lipstick should never be forgotten.

Q. What about blush?

A. Blush is terrifying when applied too heavily in the wrong color. Look for something that just adds a bit of natural glow. The light cream blushes blend in beautifully, and look wonderful worn under powdered mineral make-up.

Q. What type of eyeliner do you recommend?

A. An eyeliner should glide over the upper lash line. I've found that a cake eyeliner mixed with water and used with a brush is easy to use for almost everyone. The new gel liners are great too. They should last all day and not flake or smear. Compliment the tones

in the eye with a neutral color like charcoal, a warm brown or deep plum. A mascara in a similar hue helps rim the eye with subtle color. For the lower lashes I like a smudgy pencil in a soft color like taupe or khaki, not too dark if under eye circles are a problem. Don't even talk to me about black, except for mascara.

Q. What about eye shadow?

A. I like neutral shadows to finish a look, and used skillfully they can add dimension to the eye. Too much emphasis on eye shadow is a waste of time, unless you think it fun to use your eyelid as a canvas for painting a mural. Quality is important, though, because you want your shadow to last. Use an eye shadow primer if your days are long or your lids oily. Beware of red-based tones that make your eye look bruised. Avoid noticeable color unless it is right around the lash line or in the outside corners. Softening the hard edge of eyeliner with a bit of smoky shadow is pretty.

Q. How often should you update your look?

A. Often! New products with improved ingredients are always becoming available. Even if you fall in love with something, if you use it indefinitely it will start to look stale. If a favorite color is discontinued, as is often the case, branch out. The most important thing to update regularly is your lipstick.

Q. Why lipstick?

A. Lipstick can define an age or an era. I will carry the same basic concealer, eye make-up and blush for a number of years, but I update the lipstick colors in my line every single season.

Q. Should you vary your make-up with the colors of your clothing? Seasonally? How about going from casual to dressy?

A. The answer to all of the above is yes. Remembering back to the section on color, recall the way the reds change during the seasons. A summer cherry red is not the same as a winter blackberry, a fresh spring peach or a burnished russet. Summer make-up is sheer and reflects light, winter make-up needs to stand up to the dense, smoldering color of your winter wardrobe.

Changing from work make-up to weekend make-up is refreshing. Weekend make-up can be applied with a lighter hand, just the "feel good" basics. I sell a lot of what I call "Saturday lipsticks," glosses that look good with just a touch of eyeliner. Brush on your powder sunscreen and you are good to go. Evening or party make-up is your chance to play up your dramatic side with deeper tones and a touch of gleam and glitter. Just remember that artificial lights at night can be harsh, so no strong lines, and don't forget to blend well.

Q. What should I look for in choosing a make-up artist?

A. Every face has its challenges, and a make-up artist should be innovative when it comes to solving problems. They should be kind, responsive to your concerns, have great flair and love their work. My instinct is to hire someone who works in natural light, because that is important to me. On the other hand, I hesitate, because advice like that is too limiting. Ask for referrals. Working with someone talented will be well worth the investment. You should be able to purchase the make-up directly from the artist. If the prices for their products are outside your budget, ask for a palette of colors you can match up elsewhere. Just be clear up front that you understand their policy.

Q. Is there anything I can do to reverse the signs of aging on my face? What about the things like botox and injectable facial fillers like Restalyne?

A. Always protect your skin from photoaging with sunscreen. I'm not a dermatologist or an esthetician, so I only want to comment on the areas I've had direct experience with. I've never tried any of the injectables, and I've seen mixed results on my clients. I can just imagine asking my homeopathic physician if I should try botox. She would probably faint.

MORE ABOUT LIPSTICK

One of the things that sets me apart is that I am an absolute lipstick fanatic, a lipstick Diva, an Empress of all things lipstick. I am embarrassed to admit how many different varieties of lipsticks, lip glosses and lip liners I carry. I will search for the perfect lipstick for my customers, and then try to carry it forever, even if they are the only ones who will ever wear it. It is ridiculous.

There is something soulful about lipstick. Like the color red, it connects to the essence of your sensuality. When a lipstick is exactly right, it transforms a woman. It is hard to believe that

less than two inches of space matter so much in such a vast universe, but lips do.

Lipstick is sexy. Lips are just oh so sexy, and to define their luscious shape, you need a lip liner. Forget the dark lined lips of the eighties, and just remember to outline the shape of your little beauties. Use a color similar to the natural color of your lips, or choose one related to your lipstick. Liner helps your lipstick to stay in place, and you can fill in your lips with a soft pencil for longer lasting color. You can change the color and look of a lip gloss or lipstick by changing the color of the liner. At the moment, lip liner and a sheer but richly pigmented gloss is my personal favorite.

If there is a dark side to my lipstick universe, it is that some types of lipsticks can cause the lips to dry out and peel. Even if your lipstick is emollient, if you suspect dry lips might be caused by your lipstick, it isn't your imagination. Through trial and error, I've found that pigments in certain lipsticks are the culprits. Switching to a different product line helped. It might seem like a hassle for you to pursue finding a lipstick that doesn't negatively affect your lips, but if you persevere, you'll find something that works. I promise.

Make-up, wonderful art for the face, is readily available, affordable and gives you an immediate lift. It is expressive and personal, and the way you choose to wear it is a reflection of your spirit.

Chapter Fourteen

hair

⋈◇⋈◇⋈◇⋈◇⋈◇⋈◇⋈◇⋈◇⋈◇⋈◇⋈◇⋈◇⋈◇⋈◇⋈◇⋈◇

THE PLEASING FRAME

Looking back at photos of ourselves over the years, studying our hairstyles bring back the same kind of memories as reading an old journal. We can tell by our smiles when we were feeling confident, and we can watch our evolution like a road map of our life adventures. I was studying a photo of my hair taken twenty years ago, when the cut and color of my hair made it look like a sleek, dark pelt. No way would I have been comfortable with the messy, wild, sensuous shape of my hair now. Short hair was a good look for me in my thirties, just as I appreciate the softening effect of the style I wear now.

How our hair looks affects our confidence and our sense of self. We all strive to do the best we can with what we have. When I first sit down with a new client, questions about hairstyle and color top their list. As soon as I complete their color analysis, I'm ready with suggestions about color, because the harmonizing effect of the hair that frames your face is intimately related to the appearance of your skin tone.

Inspiration for a new style means discovering what my client's spirit is longing to express. Together we explore the options that will shape her choices. Sometimes the next step is as simple as a recommendation for a new stylist. Change can be dramatic or a subtle evolution over a period of time. Real life isn't a makeover show, where the stylist whizzes in and makes you perfect for the camera. You get to go home to deal with the flat iron and roots.

When a new client hires me, she is ready to make a change and eager for my advice. I learn more from the people who aren't my clients about the assumptions that hold women back, than I learn from my clients. When I meet someone for the first time I often wonder: What is the story behind this nondescript head of hair with no discernable style? Is the owner new to town and unable to find a good stylist? Usually the answer is that she is afraid to make a change from a style that suited her long ago, and her fear has left her paralyzed, frozen in time, afraid to move forward.

When I meet someone for the first time I often wonder:
What is the story behind this nondescript head of hair with
no discernable style?

Below are some of the explanations I've heard:

⊙ I'm afraid if I get a bad cut it will take forever to grow back.

⊙ My husband (or boyfriend or kids) likes my hair long (or short or dark or light).

⊙ I'd like to have something new, but I don't want to spend much time styling it.

⊙ I've been with my stylist for years. If I try someone new and want to come back, I'm afraid it will be awkward.

⊙ If I change from the (same) youthful style I've had forever to something more mature and elegant, I'm afraid I'll look like one of my mother's friends.

Do any of these reasons sound familiar? When I first met my realtor Yvonne, it drove me crazy that she wore no lipstick and had her hair slicked back in a pony tail. As we drove from house to house looking at property, I pondered why such an attractive woman, a former flight attendant, would want to downplay her beauty and look so nondescript. With great difficulty, I actually managed to keep these questions to myself.

Not long after we closed the deal on a house, Yvonne got a chic new haircut. Over lunch, I asked her what inspired the change.

"I wore my hair in a pony tail for a year or two, telling myself that "simple" worked for me. Maybe I just wanted to be sure I was taken seriously. Then one day I looked in the mirror and decided I looked boring, just too plain Jane, that I needed something more exciting. I was ready, and spending the time blowing it dry and styling it each day is no big deal."

When I asked my longtime stylist Jim O'Keefe what words of advice he had for my readers, he said that the biggest issue he faces is getting his clients to be realistic about the amount of time they are willing to spend on daily styling. *"When someone shows me a look they like, they need to understand that if they want their hair to look like the photo of the model in the magazine, there will be some effort involved. If they are too busy or a low maintenance kind of person, then they should choose a style that works easily with their type of hair."*

"Hair color is another challenge, especially covering gray. Some of my clients are adamant about keeping their hair their original color even when it doesn't work for them anymore. We have lots of techniques that create a more subtle effect, like using a mix of low lights and highlights so there is variation in the color. You have to be realistic about hair color, though. Not just the regular upkeep that is required, but knowing that the color fades, changes and will always grow out. Hair color doesn't permanently change your hair from one color to the next, it only alters it temporarily. It is an ongoing process that needs to adapt and change to your needs and the needs of your hair. Keep in mind that too much processing causes hair to lack luster and vitality. There are ways to add shine back, including conditioning, products and styling tools. If that

doesn't work, you've gone too far, and you need to back off."

Even though I'm not coloring my own hair at this time in my life, I admire great hair color. All those gorgeous highlights my blonde friends get greatly enhance their appearance, and I am fascinated by the creative and inventive ways that color can pop and add dimension to a style.

Find a skilled colorist, but respect that all color processing has limitations. I'm sensitive to how my hair color looks next to my skin, but just because that bothers me doesn't mean it will bother you. Having gray hair may bother you more. You'll never know until you try. Long, short, straight, curly, tousled, sleek, colored, natural, simple, glamorous, easy, whatever works for you, find a stylist you trust and let them guide you. An exciting change can lead you to discover something new about yourself. Take risks and experiment. Hair grows back. Respond to your inner self and adjust to the changes in your hair over time. Look for a way for your hair to express who you are in the moment, and reflect all the ways you are *Growing More Beautiful*.

"I liked how my premature gray looked on me, but I got tired of being asked if my young daughters were my grandchildren. You're right, I probably got twenty compliments for every "granddaughter" question, but I still couldn't take it. The negative comments are the ones that stick." Val

"When I was going through chemo, Jennifer started wearing a wig to encourage me to wear mine. She actually looked pretty good with auburn hair, and it was a fun change from her natural gray. One night we went to the movies wearing them, and we realized we finally had the dream hair we fantasized about in high school. Mine was long and thick, and Jen's shag was silky and not frizzy. But we couldn't wait to throw those stupid things away." Leslie

Part Eight   GLOW

one brush stroke

JANUARY 10, 2 P.M.: I'm getting over a cold, and I'm tired. When I arrive at
my painting location a chill wind is blowing. Dark clouds blot out the sun, and the
surrounding hills and dormant trees are dull in the winter half light. The other painters
are grimly setting up. I give myself unqualified permission to jump back in my car and
drive home. I sigh. I'm here. I think to myself that if I only make one mark on a piece
of paper, one brushstroke, I'll feel better. The tightness in my chest will lessen. I put
on my coat, and add a fleece hat over the hood of my sweatshirt. There is a chance
the wind will blow the clouds aside enough for the sun to break through.

And that is exactly what happens. An hour later, we are rewarded by the sight of
the vibrant, velvety emerald green of a Northern California winter. The shadowed sides
of the hills are a cool purple, the valleys below lit by the sun glowing lemon yellow.
A pinkish mist rises from the damp grass. Tiny dots of moisture glisten and sparkle
where they have collected on the bare branches. I wrap my hands around a cup of tea
from my thermos, and feel exhilarated as I breathe it all in.

As you reach this point in the story that is really about the art of *Growing More Beautiful*, you may be inspired, but you may also feel overwhelmed. Update your closet and your lipstick every season? Create a collage, a budget and a plan? Somehow find the time to shop not only the department stores, but smaller galleries and boutiques as well? Look for shoes that are not only comfortable but reflect your spirit?

Who has time for all of this? Isn't life complicated and demanding enough already?

CREATING BALANCE

Give your appearance the attention it deserves, and over time it will assume a balanced place in your life. When clients first begin working with me, they are often timid and unsure of our success. When we start to find clothes that look wonderful and fulfill the needs of their lifestyle, their enthusiasm grows. Suddenly the time they spend shopping yields successful results. Occasionally they go a little crazy, shopping past the point of "need" and continuing to buy clothes and accessories for the sheer fun of it.

Over time it all evens out. Some of my clients discover a true passion for fashion, and continue to spend time finding creative ways to indulge it. Others find strategies to get the most done in the least amount of time. All would agree that a certain amount of knowledge, be it about color or style, goes a long way.

Whatever role caring for their appearance now plays in their lives, all will tell you that it helped to devote some time in which they focused on getting their needs met. Andy put it this way:

"I love not spending so much time thinking that I should be beautifying myself by going into stores. I often had this underlying thought that I should be shopping, pulling myself together more and noticing what is in style. And yet that world has often made me anxious and ill at ease. Did I buy the right thing; will a better thing be in style next month; should I buy this or that? The choices were so hard, and after a purchase, I was uncertain I had made the right decisions. Now, armed with information and an understanding of my style, that uncertainty and

distraction are gone, and my focus has shifted to more
present and satisfying thoughts."

If you ignore something, it will continue to loom large in your life. It is an essential part of our human experience to want to express ourselves visually. Your spirit isn't willing to take no for an answer.

Not every moment of caring for your appearance will be pleasurable or rewarding. You will still have periods of your life when you are too busy to deal with any of it. You will have bad shopping days where nothing is right. Learn to pick and choose how you spend your "beauty" time. Don't force yourself. Watch when your energy is refueled and when it is drained. Meander down the path that feels right for you instead of struggling uphill. Fatigue is a message that the load has become too heavy. When pleasure deserts you, find another route.

Energy is renewable when you do things with flow. I am not a physically robust person and don't have a lot of stamina, so I use "going with the flow"

to my advantage. How else would I be able to run a business, write a book, paint, and somehow look pulled together from my earrings to my shoes? Energy isn't finite, and you can refill the well with how you choose to replenish and nourish yourself.

It's wise to create a rhythm that allows for breaks when you don't need to think much about your appearance, letting yourself coast for a while on your recent efforts. The seasons in fashion create natural cycles of focused attention and time to enjoy the results. There is a frenzy of fashion activity between back-to-school and the December holidays. Then most of us have the option to go into fashion hibernation until the blossoming trees stir us to wear something more colorful, and the spring fashion cycle begins. Once your needs are met, winter and summer are the natural seasons to take a break. In July, department stores try to lure you in with "pre-season sales" because they need your business. But shopping doesn't need to be a year-round activity for

Meander down the path that feels right for you instead of struggling uphill.

you. We should train the stores and not allow them to train us. Find times to pause and refresh yourself with other creative projects, or just go to the beach. Give yourself some time to let your inner earth lie fallow.

HUNGRY AND SATISFIED

You may find yourself wanting to spend *too much* time on your appearance. Ask yourself: Are you constantly ravenous for the hit that buying new clothing provides? Do you beautify yourself to the point that you end up feeling less beautiful? The giant

maw of beauty perfectionism begs to be constantly fed. Our consumer culture counts on you feeling like you are never perfect enough.

I know from personal experience how wanting to be beautifully dressed can suck you into feeling compulsive. When I look through my journal, I see there is a moment every season when I feel myself teetering on the brink of too much involvement, of squandering too much time, money and energy. My work asks that I throw myself head first into the raging fashion river, and there are times when I question if I am being sucked under by the current.

I want to stay true to my personal values and priorities, so I need to step back, calm myself down and reassess. Spending too much money on clothes will make my life difficult and unpleasant. Knowing I am in this for the long haul helps me stay focused, as does remembering that next season I will want to do it all again with great gusto and enthusiasm. Even if money weren't an issue, it isn't satisfying to have more clothes than you have days to wear them. Just as it feels good to eat when you are hungry and stop when you are satisfied, too many clothes can be like too much rich food and make you queasy.

"Every time I go on a trip, I feel anxious. I try to calm my fears by creating the perfect wardrobe. I run around in a frenzy, usually going against what is in the stores during the current season." Nina

Beauty "dollars," whether they are in the form of time or money, need to be spent in a way that will enhance your well-being. On the other hand, being on a clothing "deprivation diet" will destroy your ability to feel good about yourself. A craving, and our ability to satisfy it, is one of the most delightful aspects of human nature. Nurture the cravings you have to look beautiful. Fan the spark of interest you feel into a glowing flame. Let it light you up and energize you to put in the time necessary to move forward. What is the point of eating chocolate if you don't crave it? Half the pleasure is anticipating the way the lovely substance will taste as it melts on your tongue. You can be trusted to find your balance.

One thing I've learned about creating balance is that the results are usually uneven, the opposite of a serene yoga pose. We *grow* and learn in a messy and inexact way. To live a creative life, you need permission to do things poorly.

NOURISH YOUR ARTISTIC SELF

It is a perfect October day. Our painting group has set up at a local pumpkin patch. The Sonoma County hills glow in the late afternoon light, and the colors on my canvas are warm and rich. The only problem is the silly looking pumpkins that populate my painting. They look more like oranges, a helpful painter pointed out. No, basketballs, decides another. They are right, and I am disappointed, my lack of accurate drawing skills spoiling the painting.

A friend comes over the next day and when she sees the painting she exclaims, "Oh, how beautiful. I adore pumpkins, what a glorious painting!" and proceeds to tell me all the things she loves about it. "Aren't you bothered by the shape of the pumpkins?" I ask. "They look like…" "No," she insists, "The painting is beautiful."

Several years later I am standing on a neighborhood sidewalk one cloudy March afternoon, attempting to paint a huge saucer magnolia tree that was in full bloom, a shimmering sea of lavender and magenta against a flinty gray sky. In my excitement I haven't thoughtfully laid out my composition, and now the painting is not going well. A mother pushing a stroller walks past, compliments my work, and tells me how much she wishes she could paint, that she has no talent, no time.

As she walks away, I look at my painting in progress, already destined to be on my tall stack of paintings that don't quite work. I think to myself that the only real difference between me and that young mom might be my willingness to be uncomfortable and my longing to be a painter. Talent has less to do with it than the fact that her longing took her in another direction, towards motherhood.

In the fifteen years I have been painting, I have often felt lost, confused, puzzled, hopeless and frustrated. Yet I have never let the intense feeling of awkwardness and incompetence stop me for long. I have continued to make my way as an artist because my desire to work with color somehow overtakes the constant ineptness I feel as a painter.

That, and the sense of rightness I feel as I am doing it. Another layer to *Growing More Beautiful* is to let yourself engage in the color and creativity you have been longing for. You may, like the woman with the stroller, insist you have no talent or time, but once you get past this initial hesitation you will be amazed by what happens. Whatever your passion, know that caring for that aspect of yourself is part of the bigger picture.

You don't need to dedicate yourself to becoming an artist to engage in a more creative and colorful life. The difference between making one brush stroke, writing one word or playing a single note of

I have continued to make my way as an artist because my desire to work with color somehow overtakes the constant ineptness I feel as a painter.

music and doing nothing at all is as vast as the entire universe. People sit with so much fear and longing, wanting so much to participate, but find every reason not to dip their toe into the vast ocean of creativity. Dipping one toe in doesn't mean you have to swim the English Channel.

If you are longing for more, ask yourself what is stopping you. Is it time? Or does your inner critic have too tight a grip? Over the years, I've watched my fellow painting students drop out and disappear, usually with an excuse about their other commitments. I suspect they never gave themselves time to get over their awkwardness. It is uncomfortable for otherwise capable adults to do something they are not good at. One of the greatest skills you can develop is the tolerance to be a beginner.

Create small, accessible ways to be involved. You need a jar of colored pens at your elbow more than you need a studio. Making a collage doesn't require drawing skills and the materials are easy to come by. You might find that a commitment to a weekly class provides structure and camaraderie. Allow yourself to partake without needing to see a result. If you feel anxious or awkward, find a good teacher who is compassionate and nurturing. The same holds true for any image professional you hire.

You may already do many inventive and expressive things in your life, perhaps scrap booking, gardening, cooking, knitting, sewing. You may already be nuts for fabric and jewelry. Yet if part of you is longing for something more, from time to time try flipping a switch from being creatively task-oriented to just focusing on looking at what is around you. Spend an hour outdoors for no other purpose than just seeing. Try walking around your neighborhood with fresh eyes. A camera can enhance the experience as long as you are not focused on taking a good photograph.

Your beauty is fed by moments such as these. As you take in your environment, you will experience your beauty as a part of the same beautiful world that surrounds you.

The skills you develop as you move toward living a more creative life are the same skills you need for *Growing More Beautiful*: Learning to see, quieting the critic and having patience with the process.

Here is a letter I received from an art therapist at an acute care psychiatric medical care unit. About her work she says: *"In art therapy my focus with the patients is on playing and experimenting with colors and shapes. Patients always respond well and are surprised and pleased with their creations. It is so much fun watching the process and the amazingly different responses. Getting interested in colors twenty years ago was what I call my 'path to self-confidence and self awakening.' I went from living with the belief that no one in our family is creative, to understanding through my continued interest and experimentation with colors that creativity abounds in everyone. In addition, the study of colors and understanding the uniqueness of one's spiritual essence was, as I reflect, one of the best gifts in my life."* Sarah E. Bertsch-Johnson, M.A.

THE POWER OF INTENTION

Growing More Beautiful offers you an opportunity to create the world you wish to inhabit. Through your conscious choices, you can create an environment where you will thrive. Critical, negative and perfectionist thought patterns are so pervasive that the best weapon to fight back these demon triplets is with the power of intention.

Until recently, whenever I looked at my paintings, I felt a lingering disappointment. No matter how pleasing the colors, to my critical eyes the shapes that I had drawn always looked immature, childish and undeveloped.

Then, during a critique session at the end of a weekend workshop with Joan Hoffmann, the author of the workbook, *Paint With Intention*, we were asked to talk about our paintings in light of our intention. I shared that my purpose was to engage people through color, to have them feel a connection to the world around them and to sense they were part of the same colorful world. As I said those words, I stood back and looked at the grouping of nine paintings I had completed during the workshop, and saw clearly that I was accomplishing what I set out to do. I finally understood that while I have spent time in drawing classes, it has never been my objective to draw with exactness and create representational artwork. If that had been my intention, I would have taken an entirely different path as an artist, sought out different instructors, and chosen studio subjects instead of painting *en plein air* where atmosphere and light are all-important.

It helps to apply the same conscious intention to your self-image. If you aren't clear on your intention, then you will be bandied about like an unmoored boat, lost in the strong current of others' opinions and their own projected self-criticism and lack of confidence. Over and over you've heard me repeat the importance of choice, but the basis for your choices is your intention. What is your intention about your appearance? Do you want to look perfect, ageless? Of course not, you say. But check your actions and your self-talk.

It is my intention to clothe my spirit, to feel expressive and comfortable, and continue to discover how much more beautiful I can become. In order to feel confident with my choices, and to be clear what is and is **NOT** my intention, I made myself a list. It is **NOT** my intention to:

- Look younger
- Do all I can to slow the aging process
- Erase any signs of aging
- Be in the best shape of my life
- Wear only current fashion
- Impress as many people as possible
- Intimidate anyone
- Inspire envy

The list of things that are **NOT** my intention are the opposite of the promises that scream from every magazine and TV talk show: **Stop the Aging Process!** and **Be in the Best Shape of Your Life!** There is nothing wrong with appreciating the things that come easily. If you have a body type that loves a good workout, go for it, take pleasure in getting into great shape. Just remember that each of us has been blessed with our own unique gifts.

I guess the intentions that top my list like **Enjoy the Process!** and **Stay in Balance!** don't make for such sexy headlines. But I am clear about what matters to me.

It **IS** my intention to:

- Feel comfortable in my body
- Enjoy all sensual pleasures including movement and eating well
- Have fun with fashion instead of being a slave to it
- Develop my passion for fashion as an art form
- Connect with like-minded people
- Reach out to inspire and encourage others
- Be courageous about my choices
- Be patient, kind and gentle with myself
- Be mindful of staying in balance
- Let myself be everything I've always wanted to be
- Look beautiful (by my own definition)

As you make your way along the path of your intention, perseverance is what will get you there. On the odd occasion when a shopping day with a client turns into a fruitless search, we always have the choice to keep going or give up. Without exception, whenever we decide to continue to move forward toward our objective we ultimately find satisfying results.

I never make promises about what we will find on a shopping trip. I can't. As the saying goes, "I'm a beautician, not a magician." So much depends upon my client's intention and willingness to try something new, to take a step toward the unknown. There are always factors beyond our control in addition to the fashions that fill the stores on any given day.

I had a memorable phone call one day from a woman I'll call Debbie. Debbie lived in a small coastal town, and the list of obstacles that kept her from finding clothes was long and detailed, including low income, disabilities, being short and overweight, with no alteration person nearby. Still, she had somehow tracked me down and was calling for my help. We discussed all the ways we could approach her challenges. After a lengthy conversation, Debbie said the one and only thing that meant we wouldn't be working together: "*I don't want to risk getting involved in doing this only to have it turn out that finding clothes is still impossible.*"

Life is not laid out like a road map. We always think of results as being linear, but they usually unfold, layer after layer, like the petals of a flower. When Debbie is willing to take the next step, a thousand possibilities will unfold for her. Until then, the bud of her beauty will stay tightly closed.

People's willingness to go to great lengths for help has amazed me. In the years following the publication of *Clothe Your Spirit*, I have met a lot of determined people. One young woman wanted me to help her with her closet, so she loaded up all her clothes in her car and drove to San Francisco from Fargo, North Dakota. I've been moved and inspired by people's courage, not necessarily by the big gestures, but by their sheer willingness to be exposed and vulnerable. It takes real grit to stand up to old patterns of belief and stop questioning the right to take care of themselves in this way.

CREATE YOUR WORLD

It might take a community of like-minded people to get you where you need to go. But why not create a world where you are the most beautiful thing in it?

Together we can create a nurturing environment where beauty can flower. You need to do your part to grow your own garden. It is easy to attract like-minded people when you are living in your essence. They will find you, and you will find each other. Women have an age old tradition of gathering strength by joining together.

Turn away from the things that damage your self-esteem, snuff out your radiance and dash your confidence on the rocks. When I was in college, my roommate's boyfriend gave her a case of diet soda as a signal he wanted her to lose weight. Even at eighteen I recoiled from that gesture in disgust, begging her to get rid of someone so clearly unappreciative. In this age of "for your own good" interventions, be aware that the comments and actions of someone close to you can be even more subtle and insidious. Watch out for criticism masquerading as support. You are looking for people who inspire you to be more instead of less. Even a well-meaning stranger has the potential to say something insensitive and hurtful. If you encounter anything less than loving acceptance, step aside and let it pass by. Or take off at a gallop!

Create the world you want to inhabit. Your actions create ripples that touch everyone around you. Or as Bathing Suit Jerry would say, "*Viva la Juicy!*"

LET TIME BECOME YOUR ALLY

The people who are most attractive are both glowing and ageless. They are tuned into themselves on a deep level, and when they want to share that light with others, their caring and compassion wreathe their features. An image of the Dalai Lama comes to mind, as does the late actress Jessica Tandy, her smile radiant and luminous in her lined face. A friend went to hear Mary Oliver read her work, and when I asked her how old she thought the esteemed poet might be, she replied, "It was difficult to tell, she has that type of beauty where it is hard to even guess her age."

Beautiful has become a word whose meaning is one that I feel privileged to aspire to.

Each day brings an opportunity to evolve into the person we were always meant to become. *Growing More Beautiful* is a way of life. Let yourself live in a world where time becomes your ally instead of your enemy. Use the art of *Growing More Beautiful* to support you, a constant that helps you maintain your sense of self during tough times, and helps you celebrate and experience a sense of joy during the good times.

What I have presented here is my way of seeing, doing, being. How I care for myself is enhanced by what I have learned and by the awareness of the fact that half my life is now behind me. I hope you will expand on what I have shared, and invent your own way to care for your appearance and spirit. There is an alchemical magic in seeing how color, art, fashion, and your own personal growth all stimulate each other. Life

Together we can create a nurturing environment where beauty can flower.

expands when what you create speaks to you and fills you. If you are a pioneer in other aspects of your life, think of beauty as yet another frontier. Use this book as your field guide. Learn to adjust your mirror to find a more pleasing reflection. Turn off the television and the *People Magazine* in your mind and look for your own source of meaning.

Take it gently. Who you are and what you do is more than enough. You are perfect. And beautiful. You will be growing even more so, and I wish I could see it. But somewhere I'll be watching, and cheering you on.

epilogue

September 27, 5 P.M.: We set up our easels at the Wawona Tunnel overlook. The view into the Yosemite Valley below stretches for miles. I have absolutely no idea how to paint something so vast. I am intimidated by all the great artists who have come before me to paint and photograph this breathtaking view. What could I possibly add to it? I sit on a stone wall for thirty minutes, trying to figure out how to begin.

At 6:45, it is getting dark, and in the fading light, we can barely see our canvases. Then there it is, the promised Alpine Glow. The first tinge of pink strikes the top of El Capitan. It magically leaps from peak to peak, lighting up Half Dome, Sentinel Dome and all the surrounding mountaintops. It is miraculous. Orange and pink pastels in hand, I scribble and scratch madly on the shapes I had drawn earlier, lighting them on fire.

We drive down the mountain in the dark, but the rest of the night I feel lit up like a flame.

the spirit term exercise

The Spirit Term Exercise integrates how you look with how you feel about yourself, connecting in a verbal and specific way to your essential qualities. You will discover the key words that describe your essence as it relates to clothing. They will be a combination of your inner and outer qualities and will capture the essence of who you are, your spirit. At the conclusion, you will discover the key words that describe your essence as it relates to clothing. If you have read *Clothe Your Spirit* or have attended any of my seminars, you may have done this exercise before. If so, do you remember your terms? How have they changed?

Instructions: This is a lengthy exercise, but the results are illuminating. You don't have to tackle the exercise all in one sitting. Do a section of it at a time and give yourself the opportunity to mull it over. Similar terms will naturally group together. It is also amazing to see how opposites coexist. That's what makes you unique!

PART ONE

ADJECTIVES DESCRIBING PHYSICAL ATTRIBUTES

Circle any physical characteristics that describe you. Feel free to make up your own.

Overall Body Structure and Curves

CURVY	SENSUOUS	LONG	DELICATE	TIDY	ANGULAR
STRAIGHT	SINEWY	DAINTY	ATHLETIC	VOLUPTUOUS	COMPACT
PETITE	RIPE	SUMPTUOUS	LANKY	STURDY	SOFT
LUSCIOUS	LUSH	INVITING	ROUNDED	FULL	ELONGATED
MUSCULAR	TALL	STRONG	STREAMLINED	SLENDER	NARROW
POWERFUL	SMALL	ABUNDANT	FLAT	FIRM	LITHE
FLESHY	PERT	DEFINED	SLEEK	STRONG	LEGGY

Walk

QUICK	GRACEFUL	LANGUOROUS	LEISURELY	BOUNCY	BRISK
BOYISH	DIRECT	SEXY	PEPPY	SWINGING	DYNAMIC
ENERGETIC	GLIDING	SENSUOUS	UNDULATING		

_____

_____

_____

Face Shape

SOFT	OPEN	SLENDER	ROUNDED	BROAD	FULL
ANGULAR	HEART-SHAPED	CURVED	DELICATE	LONG	NARROW
RECTANGULAR					

_____

_____

_____

Mouth/Smile

SEXY	CHARMING	IMPISH	DAZZLING	MOBILE	PERT
SLOW	BRILLIANT	ANIMATED	WINNING	BRIGHT	FUNNY
SPARKLING	DETERMINED	LUSCIOUS	SLY	GLOWING	FULL
PRIVATE	FRIENDLY	WIDE	REASSURING	EASY	SENSUOUS

_____

_____

_____

Eyes

TWINKLING	GENTLE	SHARP	WISHFUL	ANIMATED	SPARKLING
KIND	BRIGHT	EAGER	CLEAR	INTENSE	DEEP
MYSTERIOUS	OPEN	SOULFUL	SOFT	SULTRY	EXPRESSIVE
HUMOROUS	MUTED	MOLTEN	VELVETY	WARM	

Nose

STRONG	PERKY	CLASSIC	ELEGANT	DRAMATIC	AQUILINE
PERT	DISTINCTIVE	UNUSUAL	ETHNIC	GRAND	CURVED

Hands/Feet

LONG	DELICATE	ELEGANT	STRONG	GRACEFUL	STURDY
POWERFUL	EXPRESSIVE	ARTISTIC	SLENDER		

Coloring

DARK	INTENSE	DRAMATIC	PEACHY	LUMINOUS	STRONG
GENTLE	WARM	ROSY	RICH	DELICATE	MUTED
COOL	VIBRANT	BURNISHED	FRESH	SOFT	SUBTLE
STRIKING	HEALTHY	QUIET	DEEP	GLOWING	CLEAR
BRIGHT	EARTHY				

PART TWO

ADJECTIVES DESCRIBING INNER CHARACTERISTICS

Circle choices from list or think up your own.

FEMININE	LIGHT	EARTHY	CREATIVE	REGAL	FRIENDLY
WOMANLY	BRIGHT	TRUE	DYNAMIC	PRINCESS-LIKE	QUEENLY
RELAXED	GRACIOUS	CLEAR	HONEST	BUOYANT	SENSUOUS
FREE-SPIRITED	SERENE	SIMPLE	COMPLEX	WHIMSICAL	RIPE
DRAMATIC	GENTLE	CHEERFUL	THOUGHTFUL	TRADITIONAL	SENSITIVE
LYRICAL	SPICY	DELICATE	OPEN	CONSERVATIVE	WISE
FLUID	LIVELY	CLASSIC	INNOCENT	SINCERE	STRAIGHT
SPIRITED	CASUAL	ROMANTIC	WHOLESOME	GYPSY	PRECISE

PLAYFUL	FRISKY	FUN	EAGER	GODDESS-LIKE	ROOTED
IMPISH	INTENSE	FUNNY	HUMOROUS	SECRETIVE	SURPRISING
ANIMATED	MOVABLE	GROUNDED	ZANY	SOPHISTICATED	GRACEFUL
CHILD-LIKE	MISCHIEVOUS	MOVING	FORMAL	FROLICSOME	BUBBLY
LIGHT	EXUBERANT	ENERGETIC	INFORMAL	VIVACIOUS	WARM
YOUTHFUL	CHARMING	STRONG	ELEGANT	LIGHT-HEARTED	SNAPPY
FRESH	NATURAL	VIBRANT	REFINED	FREE-FLOWING	STREAMLINED
KIND	STRAIGHTFORWARD				

_____

_____

_____

_____

PART THREE

RELATING INNER AND OUTER QUALITIES

Look over the two lists and see if you can find any parallels between your physical attributes and inner qualities. Who we are on the inside and the way we look on the outside is intimately related. Examples of words that describe both inner and outer qualities include: _dramatic, vibrant, soft, warm, gentle, deep, cool, glowing and bright_. List any terms you especially like:

_____

_____

_____

PART FOUR

SPIRIT TERMS

Step One

Look over the fashion terms below and see how they correspond to the words chosen from the first two lists. Which ones really feel like you?

Step Two

Thinking of the clothes you currently own, what makes an outfit a favorite? Are they *soft, easy, flowing, classic* or *dramatic*? How about *playful, spunky, elegant, relaxed, unusual?*

Step Three

Think of your terms in combination with each other. *Romantic* takes on a different meaning when used with *sensuous gypsy* or *classic innocence.* The individual combination is what describes your

uniqueness. Think of your terms as related, relative terms. Together they create a unified whole. Look for the balance of opposites: *Yin/Yang.* Some adjectives describe more outgoing aspects of your nature, others look inward and are more thoughtful. Be sure to include a term for your essential femininity like *sensuous, scrumptious, womanly, gamine.*

Step Four

Choose your favorite terms. Four or five is about the right number. These special adjectives are your "home base." You can always play with other words that attract you or describe a current look in fashion.

Circle choices from list or think up your own.

SOPHISTICATED	ATHLETIC	CRISP	DRAMATIC	ETHNIC	STRUCTURED
SIMPLE	CASUAL	STRIKING	PROPER	UNSTRUCTURED	FREE-FLOWING
FRESH	RELAXED	FORMAL	PRIM	EXOTIC	EARTHY
CHARMING	INFORMAL	WILD	ELEGANT	FLUID	CLASSIC
CLEAN	FEMININE	CRAZY	INTERESTING	REFINED	TRADITIONAL
STREAMLINED	SEXY	FUN	RICH	GODDESS-LIKE	STURDY

DELICATE	SENSUOUS	TAILORED	SOFT	FORWARD	RUGGED
ROMANTIC	GRACEFUL	CONSERVATIVE	BOLD	EDGY	DISTINCTIVE
LUMINOUS	LOVELY	PLAYFUL	SUBTLE	ARTY	EASY
DARING	SLEEK	NATURAL	SPICY	ANDROGYNOUS	UNIQUE
HUMOROUS	NONCHALANT	INVENTIVE	SPORTY	FUNKY	TRENDY
ORIGINAL	UNUSUAL	GLAMOROUS	FIERCE	IRREVERENT	FLIRTY
FEMININE	GAMINE	STRAIGHTFORWARD			

Choose four or five of your favorite terms and list them below:

_____

_____

_____

Play with these different words and images until you end up with a perfect fit. Keep them in mind when you are shopping. Ask yourself if a garment suits your unique combination of individual qualities. Your spirit will evolve over time, so update your "Spirit Terms" whenever you feel inspired to do so.

First and foremost, I want to thank my husband Jerry Freeman. His encouragement to explore my creative passions allowed me to develop the ideas that became this book. His constant support kept me going during the long years of writing. His actions consistently show me the true meaning of devotion.

Without coach and editor extraordinaire Susan Bono, I'm not convinced I would have been able to finish *Growing More Beautiful*. When I was submerged in a tsunami of words, Susan was in the helicopter overhead, yelling into her megaphone that she could see the beach and I was almost there. Her genuine interest in the writing process was my anchor. When the book was complete Susan turned into an exacting and demanding editor, yanking me out of my artful cloud and demanding specifics. My readers have her to thank for the practical and useful final version.

I am grateful to my art instructors who have so generously shared their passion and knowledge. I especially want to thank Carol Levy and Joan Hoffmann.

A creative dream team brought this book to life. Terry Lockman created a book proposal that allowed me the thrill of seeing how my words looked with images. The talent of designer Nancy Campana is evident in the beauty of the finished book. Working together was the ultimate experience in creative collaboration. Thanks go to photographer Jerie Jerné for lending her artful eye and gorgeous images. Photographer Victoria Webb made my photo shoot fun, and the nudes from her Belle Aqua series take my breath away.

A big thank you to my friends and family for their support and encouragement. My mother, Lois Robin, inspires me by example to fearlessly dive in and take on the big challenges. Her delightful photographs also grace this book. My father Leonard Robin and his wife Connie always lent a supportive ear and offered encouragement. My brother Daniel cracks me up, and that helps too. Special thanks to his wife, my beautiful sister-in-law Karin Leonard, for sharing the creative struggle, and to BFF Leslie Brangham. Thanks also to Yvonne Young, Jane Bell and Carole Martin. My *Clothe Your Spirit* clients have always been my inspiration, and I am grateful to them for sharing their challenges and success stories. My assistant Daria Doherty's loyalty, dedication and cool head help keep the business on track.

The final thank you belongs to my dog Katie, who curled up in my office and kept me company during the long days of writing. Katie reminded me when it was time for morning tea (and cookies), time for lunch, time for a walk or time just to take a break and play. Thanks for taking such good care of me, girl.

I want to dedicate this book to anyone reading these acknowledgements who has an original idea they long to share or a big dream of their own. Go for it. The world is waiting to hear from you.

PAINTINGS

All paintings by Jennifer Robin

PHOTOGRAPHY

Jerie Jerné (jernesphotoart.com)
Pages 2, 8, 11, 14, 18, 29 (small image), 43, 47, 54, 58, 59, 60, 61, 64, 66, 68, 74, 75, 77, 92, 101, 103, 113, 115, 117, 142, 143, 146, 148, 150, 159 (large image), 164, 167 (small image), 172, 173, 183

Victoria Webb (victoriaswebb.com)
Pages ii, 5, 25, 29 (large image), 34, 73, 83, 85, 88, 89, 110, 165, 194, back cover

Lois Robin (loisrobin.com)
Pages 7, 78, 111, 118, 135, 149, 191, 192,199

Jennifer Robin
(see website information on page 215)
Pages 12, 100, 109, 200-201

Friends of the author
Pages 42, 53, 159, 213

Lucia Antonelli (luciaantonelli.com)
Necklaces on pages 167 and 169

Simma Chester(simmachester.com)
Bracelets and earrings page 168

Clothing photographed at Lindisima
in Greenbrae, California

Cover image: Veer

FOR MORE INFORMATION ABOUT
*GROWING MORE BEAUTIFUL: AN
ARTFUL APPROACH TO PERSONAL
STYLE* VISIT:

growingmorebeautiful.com

clotheyourspirit.com

bathingsuitjerry.com

artefulpress.com

FOR FURTHER INSPIRATION, VISIT:

tiny-lights.com

terrylockman.com

campanadesign.com

victoriaswebb.com

jernesphotoart.com

loisrobin.com

simmachester.com

luciaantonelli.com

joanhoffmann.com

innerevolution.com

THE END